Making it Happen
Want It. Read This. Get It. Simple

– FIL BIGGS –

To Sammy
Let's do this!
Much love
F.

Printed and bound in England by www.printondemand-worldwide.com

http://www.fast-print.net/bookshop

MAKING IT HAPPEN
WANT IT. READ THIS. GET IT. SIMPLE
Copyright © Fil Biggs 2016

A catalogue record for this book is available from the British Library

ISBN 978-178456-385-1

First published 2016 by
FASTPRINT PUBLISHING
Peterborough, England.

To my mother,
Thank you for being the voice of reason
whilst never holding me back.

Preface

"Ask for what you want and be prepared to get it."

– Maya Angelou

You want something? Something you want to gain? Something you want to change? Of course, you do. That's why you picked up this book, right? Or maybe you are just curious. That's how it starts. Some kind of idea that lingers around your brain, every so often filling your thoughts with wondrous images and questions. What if? We all know what it's like to want something. There are two types of things that we want. There's what we really want, and then we go get them, and then there are things we *just* want. Nothing else. We don't do anything about it. We just spend our time wanting them. This book is not for the latter.

It doesn't matter what the reason is that you picked up this book. It doesn't matter what it is you want – not yet anyway. What's important right now is what you are thinking *about* what you want. Do you think it is possible for you to have what you want? Are you willing to do what it takes to get it? Can you handle actually getting it? All important questions that we will cover on this journey together.

To get the most out of this book, you will have to do a lot of thinking to yourself. I highly recommend that whilst making your way through the pages that follow, you have a pen and paper nearby. I like to have a pen in hand and keep a folded A4 piece of paper in the back of books when I read them. Insights and epiphanies can hit you at any time. It's good to get them down whilst they are fresh in your mind. This book is bound to lead to some blasts of clarity in you at some point. Be ready when they arrive. I also recommend reading the book out loud if possible. Allow the words to travel full circle from your mind, to your mouth, to your ears, to your consciousness.

This book is part teaching and part discovery, meaning that some of the knowledge you acquire whilst reading will come directly from the text, whilst other pieces of learning will come from what you do as a result of reading it. This process requires more than just you reading through the steps I have laid out for you. It will require you to take a good look at yourself, think about things you have not thought about before, and most of all take action. I apologise in advance to all you grammar fanatics out there. There will be some horrific errors here, some of which you may have already noticed. I tend to write how I speak, and that includes starting sentences with 'and' and 'but', so you'll just have to put up with it. I care more about the message getting through to you, and less about winning any prizes for outstanding writing. So please forgive me.

Making things happen is more than just a method you can use to get stuff done. It is a way of life. This book is for those people who want to make something of themselves, something of their lives, creating a life they want. Many people live mindlessly like zombies, just taking things as they come and accepting whatever is thrown at them. They don't realise just how much control they actually have over their reality. Heck, they've probably never even stopped to think about it.

No one really tells you that life is truly what you make of it. We grow up being told what to do and how to live, but then you reach a point where you stop being told. It's all on you now, but rather than take charge and think about what it is you want and then making it happen, you go out in search of anyone and anything that might still tell you what to do. Society is great for this. It is full of 'shoulds' and 'should nots' for us to abide to. Forget these for a second, and just think about you.

What is it that you want? What do you want for your life? What kind of life do you want to live? What kind of person do you want to be? When you really think about it, all we have is time and the decision of how to spend it. As far as we know, we only get this one life, so why not start thinking about what you are going to do with it!? We all have this golden opportunity given to us. Like a box of crayons given to a child, we are free to scribble on the walls of life. Sure, you may get told off for making a mess, or not keeping in the lines, but who knows, you may just create a masterpiece, and most of all you'll love every second of making it happen.

One: Believe

"The first step before anyone else in the world believes it, is you have to believe it."

– Will Smith

Anything that anyone does starts off with a vision of some kind. Even if only for a brief moment, we see what we will do and then we do it. Sometimes this vision can be so quick, we're not aware of it enough to acknowledge it. Regardless, it happens. As humans we are blessed with the gift of imagination. This means that we have the ability to create mental images and experiences that have not happened in the tangible world. You don't have to be sat on the beach sipping cocktails to imagine sitting on the beach sipping cocktails. This special ability is part of the first step to making things happen.

Using your imagination, you can begin to create a vision of what it is you want. How big or small is up to you. It can be a vision of what you would like to do tomorrow, it can be a vision of the life you'd like to have in the next five years. The important thing is that it is something you *want* to have, be, or do, and that it is set in the future.

At this point there is no need to be realistic. If anything, *don't* be realistic. Focus purely on what it is you really want. Not what you think you should want or what you think you need, just what you want. Make it bigger, better, more. Really use your imagination to create something amazing for you. It's ok to think big. There is nothing to hold you back from just thinking about it.

You are free to dream whatever you want.

Right now you don't have to *do* anything other than envision what it is you want, so let loose. Grab a pen and something to write on. Really go wild with possibilities and push the boundaries of desire. Go for the ten out of ten event, the best case scenario, the block buster advertisement for your desired future, limited only by your own imagination.

Once you have this picture that is so desirable that you just want to leap into it, listen to these words and listen carefully.

It's possible.

Say it. Say it to yourself. Keep picturing your amazing outcome and say it. Keep saying it, and even if you feel sceptical, it will resonate with a part of you. The part of you that holds hope. The part that knows that even if the odds are against you, that even if there are multiple obstacles between now and then, there's still a chance, and the smallest chance is all it takes to turn the perceivably impossible into something that is possible.

That may seem like an outrageous statement right now but stick with it for the time being. We tend to under estimate what is possible for us, especially when it comes to making big changes in our lives. Our limiting beliefs and fear tend to creep in at this point and we begin to question our vision. Leave the comments aside for now. We will deal with them later. For now, stick with the vision of what you want. Have it clear in your mind and just repeat the statement: It's possible.

This is different from the 'YES mantras' you may have heard of. There is no expectation of you to fully believe that what you have pictured is the exact future that awaits you. All that is being asked of you is to acknowledge that the future you imagine is possible. That maybe, just maybe it could happen. Keep saying it and eventually you will really begin to feel the truth in the statement. No need to question it or critique it. Just accept the possibility of what can happen.

Try this little activity. Get into a group (ideally at least 4 of you), and each come up with a possibility you want to believe. Then go around the room introducing yourself, starting with your name and then stating your belief as if it were true. For example, if Jo Bloggs wanted to believe in himself enough to become a successful entrepreneur, he would go around saying "Hello, I am Jo and I am a successful entrepreneur." It may feel a bit silly at first, but do it enough times and it will start to feel different. It will feel possible.

Even if you're struggling with this concept, that's ok. We're going to continue anyway. You have begun a process and it will take time. Practice is key and with it you can make it happen. Before anyone can do anything, they have to believe that it is possible. You can think that it is highly unlikely or improbable, but to act on a vision shows there is a possibility of its happening. The only reason you would attempt something you truly believed was impossible would be because you *want* to prove it is impossible. Even then, you must be open to the possibility you are wrong. However, you believe it is *possible* to prove it impossible. Still with me? Take a moment to read that again if you like. In summary:

We only do what we believe is possible.
What you want IS possible.

The line between impossible and possible is so very fine. When things are very VERY unlikely, we tend to just assume they cannot happen and we mindlessly chuck the word 'impossible' at it. How many so called impossible things have been done over the centuries? Recording sound, circumnavigating the world, travelling into space, Leicester winning the Football Premier League. They were all considered impossible at one point.

That's the thing about impossible things. They are believed to be that way until someone comes along one day and makes them happen. It does not change what they were. The truth is that they were never impossible to begin with. It just took someone to realise that, stand up against the odds, and act accordingly. If you truly believe it can't be done, then you won't even bother trying. Believing that something can happen is the first step to making it happen.

It being possible doesn't make you believe it. You believing it makes it possible.

There may be things you don't have right now, but you require them to make what you want happen. You must believe in yourself to get them. When you believe in you and trust that you can get whatever it is you wish, new abilities will come your way. There are things you are not able to do right now but believe that one day you will. You will learn, you will grow, and you will develop. What may seem impossible just requires some work on your part. It requires you to work on you. Know that you can. Maybe not right now, but one day. If you keep moving forward, you will inevitably get there.

Remember, at this stage *anything* is possible as it is all occurring in your mind. As Walt Disney said "If you can dream it, you can create it." This really is a dream making process, so if you want it, imagine it. Make a note of your thoughts and feelings about what you want. This is the first part of your dream entering the tangible world. What was once just a thought, is now here and you can physically pick it up, hold it, give it, protect it, or destroy it.

Believing whole heartedly in what you want to make happen and its possibility is one of the biggest challenges of free will. Your belief will be constantly challenged on the journey you embark on. With our gift of imagination, we also have the freedom of choice when it comes to what we believe. Like a baby learning to walk, constantly falling, constantly getting up. Never believing they will never be able to walk like those around them. Knowing with the entirety of their soul that it is just a matter of time. If you can have faith in yourself to make things happen without a shadow of a doubt, then you will be unstoppable.

Rule #1: Never let a shadow of doubt enter your mind *to stay*.

How you go about making it happen may adapt and change, but your true desire must stay true to you. If it does change, then let it be because it is you that wishes it to change and for no other reason. This is something we shall address again later in the book. For now, you have your desire, your wish, your dream. It is yours and yours alone. Keep it safe and keep it close. It will be the foundation of everything to come.

In order to create the best possible outcome for what it is you want, everything you decide, deliberate, and do must be done with the presupposition that what you want can and will happen because you made it. A presupposition is a type of belief. Even if you have not reached a stage where you completely believe that what you want is definitely going to happen, in order to move forward, the *assumption* is that it is.

Presuppositions allow you to side step the doubts and make better decisions when it comes to taking action towards what you want.

Belief is a real test for some people. Remember, even if you are finding it a challenge and it almost seems hopeless, there is always another way. That's one of my presuppositions. To be so sure of something without any real evidence requires a lot of faith. Not the kind of faith you hear about in religious circles, but a faith a lot closer to home. Faith in yourself, that you have the will and resourcefulness to be a creator of whatever you wish.

When you are questioned as to whether or not what you want will happen, a true believer will say "Yes" with confidence and conviction. If this doesn't sound like you, don't worry. Another response can be "I don't know", and that's ok. Truly accept you do not know what the future holds, but don't stop there. With uncertainty comes the freedom to find out. Be curious as to what is possible.

Even if you don't know what is going to happen, enjoy the journey of finding out.

No one should be judged for what they believe. If what you want is what you want, then great! No one else can dispute that or make you feel bad about it because it's what *you* want. There is a present fear in people where it is deemed wrong to think about yourself and what you want, in fear of us looking selfish or self-centred. Yet when we always put others first, it is the self that is neglected. This makes it harder to think of others and so the process defeats itself.

For the time being, allow yourself to think about you. Just you and what it is *you* want. Think of happiness and joy as a commodity. The more of it you create for yourself, the more you can give to others. Whereas, if you give it all away, you are left with nothing. None for you and none to give. This is why you should take time to make things happen for yourself first. You can spend your whole life giving what little you can with what little you have – like Mother Teresa – or you can spend half your time creating abundance so that you can then give abundantly – like Bill Gates. The choice is down to your preference. The point being, it is not a bad thing to take care of yourself first. If anything, it is beneficial to the masses if you do.

To be selfish would be to think of you and only you, all of the time. With the mentality of boosting and growing yourself to benefit you *and* others, you move forward with an energy that grows and spreads with you. Not only will you be happy for yourself but others will be happy for you. Making things happen for you helps make things happen for others. Not always directly but in some shape or form. The correlation between your happiness and your ability to contribute to other's happiness is simple. Check out the graph overleaf:

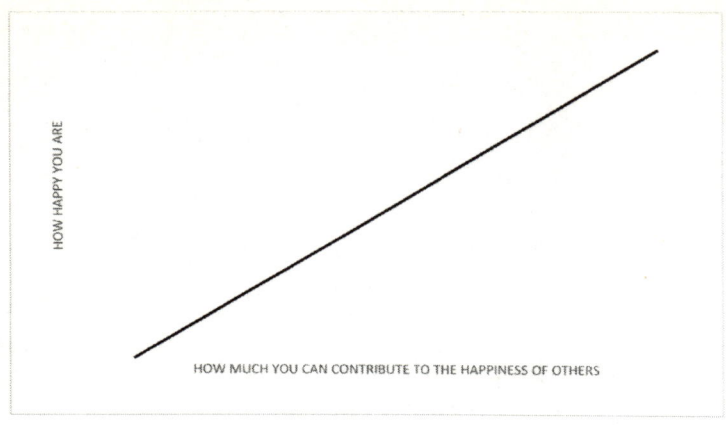

The idea you had when you picked up this book has begun to grow. The seed has been planted. Maybe it has even transformed into something more. Maybe now that you have allowed yourself to imagine beyond what you previously thought possible, the dream you have has got bigger, better, and even more desirable. It doesn't stop there. Throughout this entire process it will continue to grow and expand. New possibilities will emerge, new flowers from the seeds you have begun to sew.

With this vision of what you want and your new found belief of its possibility, we have come to the end of this stage of the process. If at any time you wish to come back and revisit this section, then please do. It will be a strong foundation for everything to come. A constant reminder of what you want will help you to keep up the momentum you gain to make it happen.

Some people take the approach of creating some kind of goal and then focusing on believing in it after. I recommend doing it as we are now, by working on the belief first. You see, if you create a goal with a limited belief in yourself and what is possible, then in turn you will limit what it is you want. You are more likely to 'play it safe' or go for what others deem as 'realistic'. This will make the rest of the journey easier but it will not make you any better and you are likely to end up with something you don't actually want very much. All because you held back.

By assessing what you believe first, you open up more doors to possibilities and this takes you so much closer to what you *really* want. We can tackle the realism and the obstacles later. For now, this is just about dreaming big, shooting for the moon, free from boundaries of what seemingly can or cannot be done. Don't worry about sounding crazy or over optimistic.

This stage is just for you. For you to open up to what can happen. What you can *make* happen.

We all have dreams. Things that we want to do, places we want to go, people we'd like to meet. This is not new. Yet very few people take the time to really think about them. These desires enter our minds to ignite our passions and motivate us for more, but soon the thoughts pass and what many people refer to as 'real life' kicks in. Trapping our dreams and thoughts in the mind, never to be released into the real world that we call life. Never to be acted on and made happen.

What is even rarer than taking the time to envision what you want is people thinking about actually doing anything about turning those dreams into a reality. They label dreams as fantasies, completely separate from reality and never allowing a connection between the two. They forget that every single thing that has ever been created by anyone, started with a vision of some kind. Reality begins as fantasy. Dreams turn into experiences.

This process of allowing yourself to explore the realms of imagination is just the first step of making things happen, but it is a step forward nevertheless. Congratulations having taken it. You are now one step closer to making it happen. Take a moment to digest everything you have learned so far. Let it resonate and expand in your mind. Then when you are ready, move onto the next stage where you will take the dream you have created and turn it into an outcome to be worked on. Project: Make It Happen starts now.

Something to think about:

- You can dream/imagine whatever you want.
- What you want *is* possible.
- You must believe first.
- Don't allow doubt to stick around.
- Enjoy creating the future.
- The happier you are, the more happiness you can contribute.

Two: Outcome

"You are capable of more than you know. Choose a goal that seems right for you and strive to be the best, however hard the path. Aim high. Behave honourably. Prepare to be alone at times, and to endure failure. Persist! The world needs all you can give."

– E. O. Wilson

Now that you have your vision and know what it is you want, it's time to turn it into a project for you to work on. The Outcome is a clear description of what it is you want to achieve. You may think that it's simply your vision you want to achieve but there is more to it than that. Your vision is made up of many aspects. In your vision there is what you have, what you are doing, and how you are being. It is these aspects that we will be pulling out of your vision in order to create your outcomes.

Firstly, look back to what you created in the last stage and decide what aspect is most important to you.

What change between now and then most stands out to you? Is it that you *have* something that you do not currently have? Is it that you are *doing* something that you are not or cannot currently do? Or is it that you yourself have changed and are *being* something that you are currently not? You may decide that there are elements of all three in your vision and this is common. The question is which one is *most* important to *you*? Which one attracts you more? Which one drives you to *do* something to make it happen?

For example, if you envision yourself getting a new car or house, then this is a 'having dream'. If you see yourself doing something different like a new job or going travelling, then this is a 'doing dream'. If you are being different in a noticeable way such as more confident, decisive, or caring, then this is considered as a 'being dream'. As stated before, a vision tends to have elements of all three but you are looking for your own preference. You could be looking to *have* a new car but it's the driving you will be *doing* that you really want, or maybe it's the way you will *be* when you have a new car that excites you. Take some time to really think about it.

Truth be told, most outcomes can be described using any of the three aspects. Just like the example before, if you are looking to get a new house, then your outcome could be to *have* a new house. It could also be to *do* the process of buying a new house, or it could even be to *be* a new home owner. There is no right or wrong way to phrase it. Whichever way sounds and feels right to you is the right way. After all, this is *your* outcome.

Deeper Outcomes

Sometimes the outcome we think of isn't as clear as it seems. We tend to think of the outcomes as surface level results. What I mean by that is, we think about the most obvious effects of achieving an outcome, not what more it could have an influence on down the line. Take a moment to think about what it is about your vision you actually want. Perhaps you dream of having a million pounds, being a millionaire, or doing a job that pays millions. However, the chances are that this is not really the outcome you are looking for. What is it about having a million pounds that attracts you? What does it *mean* to you? Money is just money until you do something with it. What would having that much money make possible for you? Would it mean being financially free? Would it mean being able to provide for your family? Would it mean being able to do more or have more choice? These are deeper outcomes.

The deeper the outcome, the more it means to you. The more it means to you, the more you will be willing to do, and the more likely you will be to make it happen. It can take some time to find your really deep outcomes, but it's worth it. This is where a coach can come in handy as they are trained to help you find what it is you *really* want. Sometimes we can think we know what we want but without taking the time to really think about it, we may be wrong. Although you won't realise until you have already spent time and energy working on it and possibly achieving what you originally set out for.

When it comes to finding your true deep outcome, the questions to continually ask are:

- What is it about this outcome that I want?
- What does this outcome mean to/for me?

- How does this outcome feel?

Remember you should still be focusing just on what *you* want. Not what you think you should want or what others want for you. Just what you want. Not what you think you *need* or what anyone else says you need, just what you want. By doing this, your outcome will stay true to you and mean a lot more to you to achieve.

Dreams are personal. Achieving them is personal. This process is PERSONAL development.

Once you find that deep outcome that feels right and resonates all the way to your core, you're ready to make it clear. Although you have broken it down to find it's true form, the clarity of it can still be hazy. In order to make it achievable, you need to know *exactly* what it is.

Result, not action.

Remember, your outcome is a result. It is not something you do to get the result. Action will get you the outcome. So if you have come up with something and it looks like an action, ask yourself what will be the result of doing it, or what do you hope to achieve by doing it? The answer will give you your outcome. This is your desired destination. There will be many ways to get there, and that is why it is more important to know the final stop at this stage.

Your final outcome is the overall thing you are pursuing. Some people *think* they know what that is but never stop to question it. Before, I used the example of wanting to be a millionaire. When you think about it, having a million pounds doesn't mean much unless you're a big fan of pieces of paper with the Queen's face on. The desirableness of it comes from the potential of what you can *do* with it. That's what counts. What would the effect of having that money be? Here is a list of potential outcomes for having a million pounds:

- Being financially secure.
- Not having to ever worry about money
- Being able to buy a house
- Providing for your loved ones
- Getting a really fancy car.
- Helping your parents to retire
- Travel the world
- Quit your job

All of these are outcomes, yet even some of them can be looked at further. The thing they all have in common is that you don't *need* a million pounds to make them happen. That is just one way you could go about it. Overall, the things we want are desirable because of the way we believe they will make us feel, or the way they will allow us to live. To find your core desires, you just need to keep asking yourself this:

Why do I want this?

Now you're asking *yourself* this question, so there is no need to get defensive. No one is attacking your dream or asking you to justify your desire. This is just an exercise of self-discovery so that you can get to the root of what it is you really want and then it will be easier to make it happen.

Clarity

When it comes to goal setting, there are many acronyms out there, created to help you really break down what it is you will be moving towards. Here are some examples:

SMART

Specific – Make your outcome detailed enough to avoid misunderstanding. There is a difference between wanting to be a millionaire and wanting to earn £85,000 a month. Like the archer, you must aim for the bullseye, not just the target.

Measurable – Decide what you will see, hear and feel when you achieve your outcome. How you measure it will decide how you will know when it has been done.

Attainable – Review your outcome and check if it feels attainable. This isn't so much a question of if it is possible, as a question of are you willing to do what it takes to make it happen.

Relevant – What matters most is that you actually want this outcome and that it is relevant to you. There is no point making an outcome to work towards if you don't really want it or it doesn't matter to you.

Timely – Goals are dreams with timelines. Give yourself a date you want to have made it happen by. This will give some urgency to the situation and demand action immediately. Bye bye procrastination.

PURE

Positively Stated – It's easy to think about what you *don't* want. Our subconscious cannot decipher between positive and negative. If you think 'I don't want to be fat', your subconscious hears 'be fat'. So give it something positive and focus on what you *do* want, like 'I want to burn fat'.

Understood – Ensure you really understand the outcome you create. Words can be misunderstood. This point is especially important if the outcome involves other people.

Relevant – Same as R in SMART (see above).

Ethical – Create an outcome that aligns with your values and morals. Does it feel like a right thing to do? Will you feel good about achieving it?

CLEAR

Challenging – If an outcome is too easy, you won't benefit as much from it. In some cases, it can be so easy that you don't even bother to do it. There's no motivation or incentive to take it on.

Legal – Don't go getting into trouble because of your outcome. Keep it legal.

Environmentally Sound – What impact will your outcome have on the environment? Keep it clean and do no harm. We've only got this world. Make it better, not worse.

Appropriate – Your outcome is likely to have an effect on more than just you and your life. Those around you will be effected to. Take this into consideration and make your outcome appropriate.

Recorded – Write it down! Memories can fade. Make your outcome concrete and tangible by recording in some way.

Using structures such as these will help you to gain a tremendous amount of clarity about what it is you want to achieve. The clearer your target is, the more likely you are to hit it. A popular analogy for this is the use of a GPS or Satellite Navigation. Say you are planning to visit a friend that lives far from you and you enter their town or city into the system. It will configure a route and you can follow it there, but once you arrive you are only in the right area, not at your friend's house. If you were to be more specific and enter your friend's postcode and house number, then the system would help you get you exactly where you want to be.

This may seem like common sense but is surprisingly not common practice. A common trait found among high achievers is the clarity and specificity around what it is they set out to do. Not necessarily the route they would take to get there, but the final destination that they will arrive at. This level of clarity leaves very little room for error. On the journey there will be questions that arise and decisions to be made. With such clarity, the answers will be just as clear and decisions can be made easily.

YOUR Outcome

This is for you. Only you. Your outcome may have an effect on others and others may even be a large part of your reasoning behind it, but for now this outcome is just about you. It is *for* you. You are you, and this life that you're living is *your* life. It is you who will take action and it is you who is responsible for making this happen. Remind yourself of that when you look at your outcome. The reason this is being reiterated is because of its importance. Others may support you on your quest to make it happen, but no one will want this outcome more than you do. Not your family, not your friends, not your partner, nobody. They may really want it too but never as much. Why? Because this is YOUR outcome.

Assuming that you have created an outcome that is true to you and what it is you want, then it should be no wonder that it is you who wants it most. Don't be surprised or deterred by this. Find great strength and ownership in it. The power to create it and make it happen is in you. It always has been and always will be. People can go for years never realizing this. Some even go their whole lives never using it. I don't believe you are one of those people. If you were, then you probably would not have picked up a book titled *Making It Happen.*

How will you know?

Getting to your final destination is one thing, but how will you know when you have arrived? If you have created your outcome using the clarity structures from earlier in this book, then the answer should be pretty straight forward. The way in which you measure your goal is crucial for recording its success. Your outcome does not have to use numbers to be measurable – but it does help.

The big question is how will you know your outcome has been achieved? Will you see it? Will you be told? Will you feel it? We experience the world through our senses and we can use them as a way of measuring our outcome. Think back to your vision, think about your outcome. Perhaps you have just been *seeing* it. So let us take it further.

Cast your mind into the future where you have achieved your outcome. What do you see? Where are you? Who are you with? What are you wearing? Build up the visuals of the image. Is it a still image or is it moving? Is it in colour or black and white? Are you seeing it through your own eyes or can you see yourself in the vision? Once you have built up the image, open up your awareness to your other senses.

What about the sounds in your vision? Think about what you can hear. Listen to the sounds around you. What can you hear? Are there many sounds? Can you distinguish between them? If there are voices, who's voices are they? What are they saying? Are the sounds loud or quiet? Is there music? Now turn your listening inwards. What are you saying to yourself? What comments are you making in your internal dialogue? What kind of tone are you speaking in?

Once you have built up the sights and sounds of the experience, focus your attention to what is happening within. How do you feel? Do not rush the answering of this question. Just allow yourself to feel it. It is easy for your logic to jump in here and reel off a list of ways you think you *should* be feeling having achieved your outcome. So don't go for the instant response. How are you feeling? Maintain the sights and sounds you have created and allow yourself to just be in the experience. It is ok if you find it a bit challenging to articulate the experience. The answer is only for you. It matters most to you. Emotions can be difficult to describe. The emotional part of our brains is on the opposite side to language and we are limited by the language we use. Let's be honest, the word 'happy' doesn't really sum up what it actually feels like to be happy, and everyone's interpretation can be different.

Being in touch with how your vision feels when it happens will allow you to better know when you arrive at it. Now you have many ways of measuring the achievement of your outcome, you can begin to answer the big question of 'How will you know?' With this answer, finish the following statement. It may not be a short answer, but it's *your* answer.

I will know I have made it happen because….

When it comes to measuring results, be sure you are measuring what you actually want to change. When it comes to getting healthy and burning fat, the majority of people talk about losing weight. Although measuring weight is a good indicator of how much mass you have it probably isn't what you actually want to change.

If I had a magic wand and gave you the choice of having your dream body but weighing ten kilograms more, or having the exact body you have now but weighing ten kilograms less, which would you choose? I am yet to have anyone choose the second option. If you aim to lose weight, the second option is the one for you, right? There is a conflict between what people want and what they measure.

In reality, when people say they want to lose weight, they probably actually mean they want to lose fat, get slimmer, tone up, change their body shape, or drop down a size or two. Whatever it is, they *really* want, *that* is what they should be measuring. Have a good think about what it is you are looking to change.

Is that *really* what you want to change? If that changed but nothing else – like your weight but not your body – would you still want it?

Values

Once you have a good idea of what your outcome is, have a think about how it aligns with your values. If there is conflict between your outcome and what is important to you, then this will lead to more challenges ahead. The biggest challenge being the fight you have with yourself when it comes to getting things done. I refer to this as 'Inner Conflict'.

A friend of mine was telling me about how he would love to get into shape but just didn't have the time. His week consisted of working, socialising with friends, watching his favourite tv shows, and sleeping. I helped him to create a schedule that would work for his routine and he said he would give it a try.

Two weeks later, I see him and ask how the training is going. "It isn't" he replied. He then went on to explain how whenever it was time to train, something came up. He had to work late, there was a meet up with friends, his favourite show was on. Even if training was planned for first thing in the morning, sleep got in the way.

It is not that my friend is lazy – at least that's not the biggest reason for his results. It is that he values other things more than getting into shape. Perhaps you've been in a similar situation where you plan to get up early to do something you want to do, something just for you, and when it comes to the day, the idea of tearing yourself out of bed doesn't even bare thinking about. What changed? You were eager, enthusiastic, maybe even excited about doing what you had planned, and now you just won't do it. What changed was your values. In fact, they didn't change. They just kicked in.

If like my friend, you value sleeping, working, watching tv, and socialising with friends, your outcome may conflict with them. If it does, then you have some options. You can assess the value of your outcome. If this result is really important to you then it will come out on top when put against other things you value, but be aware of the potential effects of this (ecology). Or you can plan for your outcome to work around, or even with your values. If being healthy and fit is important to you then training fits in perfectly. If sitting on the sofa watching tv is, then it won't. What do you value?

Wording

At this stage, your outcome will be coming together nicely. The final part in its creation is actually writing it down. How you word and phrase your outcome is very important. Language plays a large role in how we think about things. To expand on the point made earlier under the subheading of 'Positively Stated', the mind does not differentiate between positive and negative statements. For example, if you say "I don't want to smoke", the brain still registers the words "I want to smoke". If you say "I am not a heavy drinker", there are still the words "I am a heavy drinker" and these get through to the subconscious. In order to think about *not* being something, you will subconsciously think about being it.

In order to avoid these un-resourceful messages getting through, you can phrase your outcome in a positive way. Instead of saying "I don't want to smoke", you could say "I want to live smoke free." Instead of telling yourself "I am not a heavy drinker", you could try "I am sober." Avoid the 'nots' and 'don'ts'. Positively phrased outcomes better lead to positive outcomes being achieved.

Next is the tense you phrase your outcome in. When it comes to what you want to make happen, now is the most important time. The past is the path you took to get here. The future is where you are heading. Now is where the creation happens. Your outcome may seem like it is in the future but it is right now, here in the present that you begin to make it happen. Your outcome should state this so.

If you place your outcome out in the future, then this is where your mind will keep it. It can be in the very near future but it will always remain just out of reach as the future never comes. To make your future vision become a present reality, make your outcome a present that you envision. You may have come across people who say they will do something but never get round to doing it, or suggesting they will get something but it never seems to come. You yourself may be guilty of this. What is set in the future is easy to keep there.

Your outcome may not be happening right now, but it is the truth you are going to create. In fact, if you are making your way through this process, then it is the truth that is being created. To say you are *going* to do something is to delay the future. You delay it happening. This is also known as procrastination. So why wait? Start now by stating it now. If your outcome currently suggests you are going to do, be, or get something, take out the 'going'. You *are*, not you are *going* to be; You *have*, not you are *going* to have. Here are some examples of outcomes rephrased from future to present:

I am going to quit smoking. >   I quit smoking.

I am going to get a promotion. >   I am getting a promotion.

I will get round to it. >   I am doing it.

I will be more confident. >   I am more confident.

Make it present, make it true, make it real. By stating your outcome in the present, you eliminate the obstruction of time and help your mind to combine the outcome with your belief from part one. This in turn makes it stronger. The conviction of truth with which you state your outcome, also allows your mind to think and behave 'as if' it was true. This idea will be covered more in part seven, but we're getting ahead of ourselves. Essentially it means you will be able to think and take action as if your outcome is already happening, because in fact IT IS.

To recap, your outcome should meet the following criteria:

- Depth – Your outcome is what you *really* want.
- Be/Do/Have – It is something you want to be, do, or have.
- Yours – It is *your* outcome for *you* to make happen.
- Clear – Defined clear in all aspects (SMART, PURE, CLEAR).
- Knowhow – You have stated how you will know when it happens.

- Phrasing – Worded positively in the present with conviction.

Once you have done all of these, you will be left with a solid outcome that is ready to be made happen. Before then, there is a greater power that will make you unstoppable on the journey you have begun. This power comes from your reasons behind making it happen. When you and your outcome are ready, make your way over to stage three and let's get you powered up.

Three: Why

"Your problem is you know why you want to quit, but you don't know why you should keep going."

– Dr Eric Thomas

As the saying goes, "Everything happens for a reason." There is no effect without cause. The thing you want to make happen can only happen if there is a reason for it to do so. That reason is because you *made* it happen. So what is the reason for making it happen in the first place? What is the reason you picked up this book? Sure, it is clear you now have something you want and can now see it with such clarity that it is too irresistible to not go for, but why bother? In this stage we are going to look at the driving force of why it is you want this outcome.

Your 'why' is about more than just the reason for making your outcome happen. Have you stopped to think about why you even have an outcome? What is the outcome for? It is not just so you have a clear idea of what it is you are creating. You have it as a source of energy to drive you forward. Your reasoning for creating it will also do this. The idea of the outcome should ignite you inside and excite you to act. If you don't get this, then maybe you should take a look back at the last chapter. When you think about your outcome, do the edges of your mouth turn upward?

Your outcome will be in two parts. The first part is what you want to make happen. I am…, I have…, I'm doing…. The second part is your why. The whole point of the first part is so that the second part occurs. It is just as important, if not more, and that is why it is part of your outcome. In case you have not thought about this yet, we will explore it more in this stage. You have the 'what', now we work on the 'why'.

Don't get defensive.

When questioned why, it is easy for our minds to go into defence mode and begin to retaliate as if it were under some form of attack. We feel threatened somehow and there is the need to protect ourselves. Do away with this feeling and impulsive response as soon as possible. You are not under attack in any way and neither is your outcome. The answer to this question of why is for you and only you.

Your outcome does not need a justification to anyone else. It does not need to be backed up with facts or evidence. It does not require any kind of external support in order for you to want it. However, it *is* very important that there is some kind of reason for it. This reason is most important for you and it is you who will need it most on your journey.

The bigger, the better, and stronger your why is, the more power you will have to complete this quest you have started. Your why is the foundation upon which you build your outcome. It is the fuel that feeds the fire of your burning passion. It is the light that shines through your belief and projects it out into the real world. Now it may seem like your reason for wanting your outcome is obvious, but unless you've taken the time to really think about it, chances are there is more to it. The following parts to this stage require you to be *very* honest with yourself.

A reason that is true to you, can never be stopped by anyone else.

Even when you have a reason, we are going to add to it. We're going to make it bigger, better, and stronger than anything that lays ahead. Our aim is to make your why so big that it can plough through anything that gets in its way. An unstoppable force at your disposal, ready to triumph your way forward.

Want

One of the most important reasons – if not *the* most important – for making your outcome happen is that you want to. If you don't really want it to, then it would be a good idea to stop now and come back later with something you do. Assuming that you do want this outcome to happen – not just kind of want it, but *really* want it – then by all means, please continue.

Wanting your outcome is a good reason and for some people it is the only 'why' they need to make things happen. The trouble with wanting is that it is fragile and flexible. Despite their potentially epic size, they are susceptible to change. Depending on the will of a person, a want can start off so strong it can conquer all, then suddenly disappear depending on the situation.

Think back to when you were a child. Think of the kinds of things you wanted. The things you wanted more than anything else in the world. Maybe it was a certain toy. Maybe it was a type of food. Maybe it was to play your favourite game. These things may have felt so important at the time. You might have been willing to give up all your pocket money, or do all your homework, just to get it. Do you still feel that way? Most likely not. The things we want throughout our life change and for some they change often. Even if you don't ever get it, you wanting it can change. Even if you *do* get it, you wanting it can change. How often do you hear of people wanting what they can't have, or getting something they wanted and then not wanting it anymore? This is not about being fickle. This is not a bad thing. It is just something to be aware of.

It is natural for our wants to change. The world we live in, our circumstances, we ourselves, they are all ever changing. It is no surprise that our wants would change too. A want can change in a split second. No matter how much you want something. A newly found piece of information, a change in circumstance, an unexpected obstacle, they all have the potential to change what we want.

Imagine a solid gold bar is offered to you. It is valued at just over two million pounds. You are asked "Do you want it?" How much do you want it? Are you willing to give up your car, your job, your home, or even all three for it? Now imagine that you have just been informed that the gold bar is stolen and is currently being searched for by the police. Or you hear that the value of gold has plummeted below the value of paper. Or perhaps you find out there is a three-million-pound service charge to take it. Do you still want it?

Now think back to why you wanted it in the first place. It isn't likely that you've just always wanted to have a gold bar to use as a paper weight. It is more likely that you wanted the value that the bar had and what that could mean for you and your life. However, if that value, or the cost of getting it changes, you may not want it anymore or just not as much. It is because of this that merely wanting something is a dangerous 'why' to move forward with. Wanting is like the front of a snow plough or a cattle grid on the front of a steam train. It is great for cutting through the obstacle in front of it and clearing the path easily, but you need a couple of tons of horse power and weight behind it if you are going to move forward with it.

Your reason(s) must be genuine in order to have the most impact. You can spend a lot of time making up reasons in order to bulk out your why, but this is a waste. Sometimes, you cannot think of many reasons to make something happen. Sometimes you can't really think of any! That's ok. The biggest reason is still that you *want* it to happen and what making it happen will bring. This is a sign of a true authentic desire. When you do not have any other reason other than you want it, that is when you know you *really* want it. Nothing is forcing you to want it. Nothing is causing you to *think* you want it. You just do. A coach is good for exploring these wants to find your authentic desires. The more self-aware you are of your thoughts and feelings, the easier it is to find the wants that are truly yours.

More than wanting.

There are somethings we want in life just because we would like to have them. In order for your why to get bigger and stronger, you must add reasons and make them important to you. This is where your values come into play. When you know what is really important to you, you can create reasons with them and this in turn will reinforce the strength of your why.

Everybody has a particular set of values that is individual to them. These are the things that mean the most in your life and you hold them close to you. To some it is family and relationships. To others it may be their reputation and how they are perceived by others. You may value your health above all else, or maybe it is your financial status that you hold dearest.

Values come in many shapes and forms. Eliciting them can sometimes be challenging. Having a coach for this is very useful as they can ask you the right questions to explore what is important to you. It is possible to have certain values without even realising how important they are to you. If there is something you already have always had in your life such as caring parents or financial stability, you may subconsciously take it for granted and not realise just how much you value it and would do anything to keep it.

If you struggle to think about what you value, go back and take a look at your outcome that you wish to make happen. It is likely that the area or situation linked to your outcome is something you value or at least associated with something important to you. If your outcome is to do with your job, then your job may be something you value. It may not be the job itself though. Perhaps it is the idea of contributing to something bigger than yourself, or maybe it is the financial security that your job brings that is important to you.

Follow the rabbit down the hole, deeper into the core of your values. Continue to ask yourself "Why is this important to me?" or "What does that mean to me?". Doing this with a variety of different things in your life can reveal patterns. Things that may have seemed completely disassociated may actually have the same value underpinning them. Eventually we get to a point where we can't explain why something is important to us or why it means so much. It just does. It is just something we believe or choose.

Our values and beliefs go hand in hand. As stated before, the why of your outcome requires no justification, it just needs to power you through like rocket fuel to smash through the atmosphere and towards the stars. The same goes for what you value and what you believe. They do not need to be justified. The reason we explore your why is so that you better know yourself and what it is you are doing. Questions will arise on the road ahead.

The better you know yourself and why you want this, the more you will have to the questions that come.

So how do you create a reason why based on a value you have? The outcome you are going to make happen is going to have some kind of effect on you and your life. The bigger the outcome, the bigger the effect. This outcome will also have an effect on what you value. Now assuming that your outcome is in alignment with your values, then this should be a positive effect. If it is not aligned, then you may want to go back and rethink your outcome a little.

The effects that your outcome will have on your values become reasons to make it happen. Let's say your outcome involves getting a promotion at work and one of your values is providing for your family as family is very important to you. This outcome could mean a raise; a raise means you will be better able to provide for your family. So through association, getting the promotion becomes as important as providing for your family. All the more reason to get it.

Sometimes the association is not as straight forward. For example, if an outcome is about getting in shape and a value you have is family, they may seem completely separate, but there is always a link. Getting in shape could mean you looking better, healthier, fitter. This leads to you feeling more confident about yourself. With this new found confidence you are able to go for more things you want and one of those things is approaching your boss to ask if you can work from home one day a week. After all, your confidence has also pushed you to strive for more and you've been smashing company targets left, right, and centre. This allows you to spend more time with the family. The family you value so much.

Success breeds success. By achieving this outcome, you thrive into becoming better. No matter how small or how simple, each outcome you make happen benefits you and helps to make success become a habit. Another reason to add to your why list. Once you have enough reasons – enough 'whys' – then *not* making it happen doesn't really feel like an option anymore. The outcome is made important. So important that no one and nothing will be able to stand in your way.

Purpose

One of the biggest values you can link an outcome to is your purpose. Purpose is a big deal, yet it may be something you have not really given much thought. For others it is what takes up most of their thinking time. The question of our own meaning. The reason for our own existence. You could call it the ultimate why question. If you have not spent much time thinking about your purpose, the 'why' for your being here, then I highly recommend you do.

Meditation is a good tool for this. Allow yourself to become fully present and free to think. A lot of meditation is centred around clearing the mind of thought and separating yourself from what you think, but meditation can also be done simply by taking a moment for yourself in a comfortable place of peace and allowing yourself to just think about what it is you want to think about whist remaining aware of your own thought process to refrain from letting your mind wander too far off track.

One way to keep yourself centred and focused is to sit in a quiet place with some kind of intermittent sound such as a bell or chime. Nothing too invasive as to disturb the peace, but enough to get your attention. This will act as a signal to your consciousness to refocus if it has gone astray. If your thoughts are focused, then you can just continue. It is also recommended that you have a pen and paper to hand, as great insights can come out from nowhere and should be recorded before forgotten. Even if it isn't a huge life altering insight, recording your thoughts will help your mind to process them and they could potentially lead to greater insights.

There are many ways to reveal your purpose, but that is for another time – and another book. Some people find it in their day to day life, some have it find them. To some it is given, and others take it of their own. Regardless of how, it all comes down to a decision. The same way we are free to choose outcomes, we are free to choose purpose. We can have just one or as many as we like. The same way you have made the decision to make this outcome happen, your purpose is yours and yours alone. Even if your purpose is beset on you by another, it is still *your* decision to accept or reject it.

Once you have your purpose, or at least a sense of it, you are able to link any outcome to it. This makes your why incredibly powerful. This power will become very useful when you are taking action. Even if you are unsure of your purpose or don't feel it is necessary to know, that is ok. You can still create a very powerful why for your outcome using values and desire alone.

Think about the mark you will leave on this world after you are gone. Think about the effect you have on others. When you are doing what you are doing for you and only you, the power and responsibility are yours to bare alone. This brings a sense of pride and self-empowerment that you can use in your endeavours. However, you can multiply this power when you *also* do it for others. When you are doing something for others, suddenly the action becomes more important. The reason becomes bigger, and any thought of giving up seems almost selfish. Maybe the others for you is your family. Maybe it's your friends. Maybe it's just one other person who you care about dearly. Maybe it's someone who is in dire need of your help. Who it is, is up to you. They all have the power to take you further.

Benefits

A good way to build up your why is using the benefits of making your outcome happen. As discussed before, your outcome will have a knock on effect on you and your life. Like a pebble dropped into a pond, your outcome's effects will ripple out to everything around you. It will affect how you think, what you do next, the people around you, the experience you have, everything! Even if it is not a lot, it is still there.

First there are the immediate benefits. The intrinsic reward of accomplishment as well as the outcome itself. Now think bigger. What else does it mean? By making this outcome happen, you are also setting up the foundations for another. This outcome becomes the door to something else. What is on the other side of that door? What great outcomes are now made possible?

You see, one of the best things you can make happen is possibility. That is what this outcome will do. Sometimes you don't even have to do anything anywhere other than your own mind to make possibility happen. That is what you did in stage one. Achieving this outcome will be like adding a new colour to your pallet. Not only do you now have the new colour, you have a whole new set of potential colours to mix and make. Making things happen is not a one off event. It is a link in the chain reaction of life. It is the adding of thread to a string, and with each one it becomes bigger, thicker, longer, and stronger, turning it into rope that can be climbed to great heights.

Greatness is not something you are born with or given. It is built, piece by piece.

Now you may ask yourself, "Why have such a big why?". Here's why! When your why is big and true, it can take you further than you ever thought possible. When your why is big enough, you can go that extra mile, that extra day, that extra step. You can stay consistent. When your why is bigger than anything that gets in your way, doors open to you, opportunity presents itself, possibilities appear, all as if by magic, things start to go your way.

Ecology

Ecology refers to the relationship and interactions between different things and their environment. With regards to your outcome, ecology is how your outcome will make a difference in the world. Do not confuse this for thinking about how your outcome will change the whole world – even if it might. This is about the footprints that your outcome will leave behind in the making of it happen and beyond its happening.

You have already taken time to think about the benefit in order to strengthen your why. Now it is time to think of what other effects may occur. This doesn't mean creating a list of cons to balance out the pros. It means increasing your awareness of what repercussions there can and will be as a result of the project you are undergoing.

Sometimes we can get so caught up in the hype and excitement of our outcome, that all we think about is how amazing it will be and all the good things that will come because of it. This is great for positive energy and motivation, but the danger is that it can make us blind to some of the costs and unexpected happenings that also occur as a result of achieving it. The world we live in is in a constant battle of balancing itself. As Newton's third law states "For every action, there is an equal and opposite reaction." Ups are met with downs, forwards matched with backwards, progression reflected by regression.

The pairing is not always clear, and the relationship is not always on the same level. If you were the only thing in the universe, then you would not really be able to move anywhere as you experience the equal and opposite reactions of your actions. You would have nothing to move in relation to. In the world we live in, this is not the case. We are able to push down into the ground and the ground pushes back so we are able to walk, run, and jump. We are able to push back against water so that we may swim forward. We use these reactions every single day, and we mostly use them to our advantage. By identifying the reactions of your outcome, you have the ability to mitigate them or even change them.

If your outcome involves gaining, then it can be assumed that someone or something is taking a loss. This does not have to be a bad thing. It is just the process of balance.

Check out the example below:

Outcome – To sell a product you have created.

1. The Purchase

You = ££ Income

↑

Customer = ££
Cost ↓

2. Time and energy

You = Spent ↓

Customer =
Saved ↑

The exchange is imbalanced in areas and one side tends to gain, but overall the transaction is balanced. Where something is gained, something is lost. So the question is what are you losing by making this happen? Most of all, what are you *willing* to lose? In most cases it is our time and energy that are the resources we use most. With these we can create more resources to gain more opportunities. It sounds simple, and it is.

If you DO more, you can do MORE.

Now going back to your outcome and the ecology of it. Take some time to think about the world in which your outcome will happen, and what 'costs' may occur. If your time and energy is going into this, does that mean something or someone will be getting less of you? If it will cost you money to make happen, have you budgeted for it? Will making it happen have a negative effect on anyone, the environment, or part of your life? If so, is it worth it?

As stated before, this is not about creating reason not to make it happen or put you off. This is about creating an awareness so that you are better informed for the journey ahead. The clearer you are about the cost of what it is you are doing, and how much you are willing to give, the easier it will be to make it happen. These ecology checks can reveal some potential blind spots for people. It is another area where having a coach can be useful. Think about when you see a dog chasing a car. They are full on energy and motivation. They have their plan of how they will catch the car, but it begs the question: What happens when the dog catches the car? Being aware of how you will get the outcome you want is one thing. Ecology is knowing what means once you have it. Think about it.

Summary

When it comes to Why:

- Do not get defensive.
- Most of all, want it.
- Then want it more.
- Create reasons bigger than you.
- Link to your purpose.
- Add benefits.
- Check ecology.

Your 'why' is the weight behind the force of your actions. It is the power that will give you the momentum to plough through anything that gets in your way. There will be obstacles along the way - and these will be discussed in stage five – but it is your 'why' that will get you through them. It will pick you up when you fall down. It will push you forward when you are knocked back. You only need one small why to get started, but you need more to keep going.

Four: Plan

"By failing to prepare, you are preparing to fail."

– Benjamin Franklin

Any kind of force or energy requires direction in order to have motion. Without this, it can have no effect. Now that you have the destination you will reach, this is where you create the route to get there. The benefits of planning may be obvious, but the way you go about it can have a dramatic effect on your results.

Some people are meticulous and like to plan every single step in very fine detail. This is great as it makes taking action a lot easier as everything is already laid out for you and very little thinking is required later in the journey. This allows for more time *doing*. The disadvantages are that this level of planning requires a lot of time and energy, as well as information. It also leaves little room for changes in you and unexpected variables beyond your control.

At the other end of the spectrum there is the 'go with the flow' approach and the 'see what happens' way of doing things. This way of planning – or not planning – is great as it allows for great flexibility in an unpredictable environment and saves you a lot of time at this stage. The downside is that the lack of structure can make it easy to go off track. More thought is required at every stage and this can lead to procrastination.

Both ends of the continuum work. Depending on the type of person you are, you will have your own preference. You may even find there is a difference between the type of person you *are* and the type of person you *want* to be. Don't worry if this happens as the approach we are going to take in this book is a balance of both. There is a 'sweet spot' right in the middle of these two planning styles where there is a beautiful balance of structure and flow.

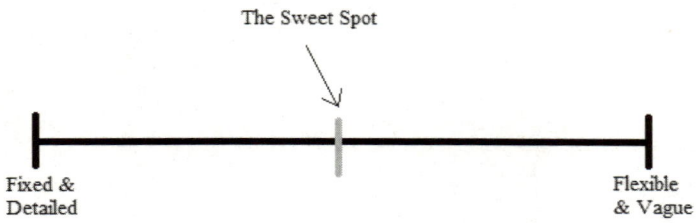

The Zoom Method

For your outcome to happen, a gap must be filled, the map drawn out, the road laid down. To do this in a way that perfectly balances detail with flexibility, we are going to use an approach I call 'The Zoom Method'. Using this technique, we will fill the gap between where you are now and where you want to be so that when it comes to making your journey, you can keep track of where you are going whilst allowing for route changes and detours.

Using this method also allows you to anticipate potential obstacles that could arise. This is covered more in part five. The aim of the plan is to give yourself a structure that supports you during the process of taking action. This is not a strict step by step guide, nor is it a vague signpost pointing in the general direction of where you want to go. It is a system for showing you the way so that no matter what happens, you have something to refer to. Even if things don't go to plan or you end up doing something completely different, having the plan to start with is still beneficial.

The big picture

At the start of The Zoom approach is the big picture. Imagine you are looking at big map with your current location and your target destination marked out with pins. A straight line connects them. With this image you can clearly see where you are and where you are going. You can also get an idea of the distance between the two. Not exactly *what* is in between them, but the 'gap' is evident.

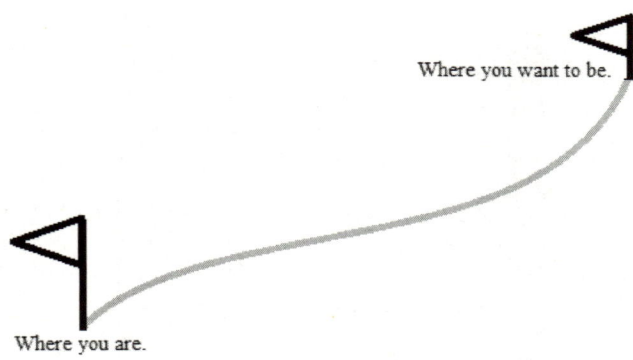

Where you want to be.

Where you are.

You already have all the information you need to imagine this image for you. You know where you currently are in your reality, and you know where you want to be – your outcome. This stage is where we fill in the stuff that needs to happen to get from one to the other. This is what you will be doing to make it happen.

1ˢᵗ Zoom

Now that the start and finish of your journey have been marked out, we can zoom in a little. As you will find with a digital map, the major cities and land marks will be named. For you and your outcome, these are the big steps that you will pass through on your way to reaching your final destination. Take some time to think about what these could be. It is likely that if you have made your outcome a big one, then it will require many smaller outcomes to be achieved in order to make it happen. This is sometimes referred to as 'goals within goals'.

There will be around three to five big milestones that must be reached in order for your outcome to happen. Overleaf is an example of this with regards to organising a party:

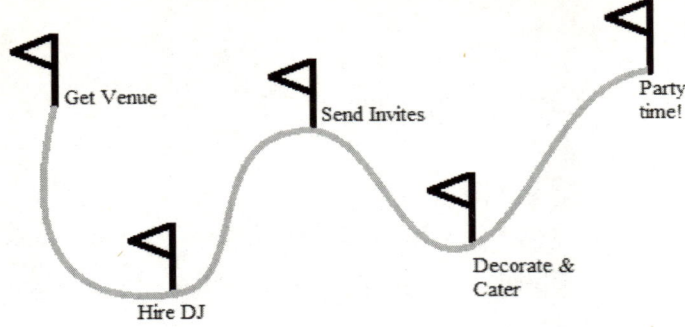

Each of the milestones will require many actions of their own. This image gives you a rough idea of what will need to be done so that you can move closer to creating what you want. The structure allows you to see the way to get to your chosen destination, and may even help you to see just how possible your outcome is. This feeling will only grow as you go on through the process.

These milestones are not necessarily necessities. They are the things that you want to have done so that you can make your outcome happen. You may choose to have essential steps in play at this stage. This is ok, but remember that this is still a rough plan of the route. It may still change later in the process. Looking back at your first zoom, you may notice that some checkpoints are needed and some not so much. Looking back at the example from before, the important steps can be marked for clarity.

Get a venue = Important
Hire DJ = Not essential but desired
Send Invites = Important
Decorate/Cater = Not essential but desired
Party time = Essential!

It is ok to have essential stages *and* desired ones. The key thing here is that you know the difference between the two early on. This will help you later on if there are any unexpected occurrences and you need to prioritise. Although each of these steps may be as important as the other, there will be an order to them. This does not mean that you cannot take an action towards more than one at a time, but there tends to be outcomes that you will want to achieve before you work on the others.

Take a moment to think about the order you want to work on your milestones. If the order does not really matter, then it is completely up to you. I recommend you do the easiest or hardest one first, depending on how difficult the overall journey is going to be. Doing the easiest first will help you to get going and build up some momentum. Doing the hardest thing first may be challenging but once done, smoother sailing awaits. It only gets easier from that point and then finishing is the easiest. Once you have your order, we will zoom in again on the first milestone.

2nd Zoom

The first milestone is an outcome in itself. Depending on how big it is, you may need to repeat the previous zoom in order to break it down even further. You will know when you have broken it down enough when outcomes become actions. By this I mean your outcomes don't need other outcomes to happen, they just need action to happen. Before you get to that stage, you want to be sure that you have the first outcome you want to achieve.

Action vs Outcome

You may be wondering what the difference is between an action and an outcome. An outcome is the result you wish to make happen. This result can likely be achieved using a few different actions. The action is what you will actually do to achieve the outcome. Here is an example:

Outcome – Have a conversation with my partner about taking a holiday.

Actions – Call partner, Email partner, Text partner, Meet with partner.

The outcome happens as a result of taking the action.

Options

Once you have your first outcome, we can then look at the possible actions to make it happen. A trap that some people fall into is coming up with an action – usually the most obvious – and deciding that is what they will do. By rushing this part of the process, you potentially miss out on other possible methods that could be beneficial to you.

Your outcome is set and you are committed to making it happen. However, the way you go about it is not. It is rare that a destination only has one road leading to it. Unless your outcome is quick and easy, there are usually many different ways to get there. You just need to take some time to look for them. Even if you end up going with your original idea, allowing yourself to explore more ways means you will have more options. This also applies to your 'big picture'. The milestones you have come up with may not be the *only* route.

The important thing is that you have where you are, where you want to be, and some ways of getting there.

Even when you think you have come up with all the different ways and actions, remember: You have not. You are only limited by your beliefs and your imagination. Having a coach is useful here, as they can assist with thinking outside the box by helping you to look at the situation from different angles. Here is an example of option listing:

Outcome: Bring in more sales for my business.

Options: Bring in more people to help sell, get a business coach, provide samples of the products, invest in advertising, research market preferences, create new innovative product, create a pop up stand at local events, hand out leaflets, create special limited offers, bring in celebrity to market brand, host taster events, bring in a consultant/mentor, provide bulk options to large buyers, and many more.

Remember, this is not a list of things you *will* do. They are just potential things you *could* do. Once you have a decent sized list (around 8 to 10, it's up to you), you can then begin narrowing it down. Start off by crossing out the one you will definitely NOT do. Not because you can't, just because you don't want to. Warning: Be aware of eliminating an option that may be hugely beneficial to you, even though you don't really want to do it. Sometimes the thing we least want to do is the very thing we need to do most. Or as Ralph Waldo Emerson said "What we fear of doing most is usually what we most need to do."

To help with this, use the model below:

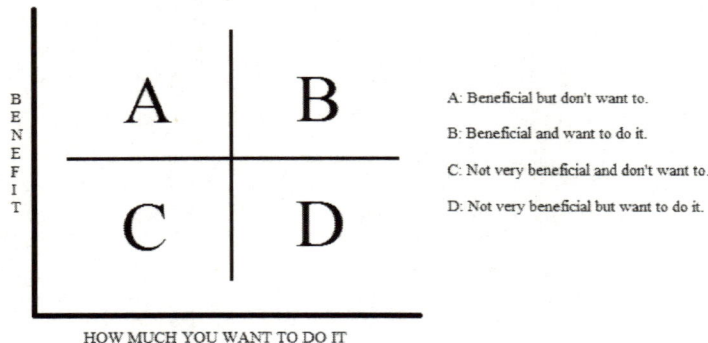

A: Beneficial but don't want to.

B: Beneficial and want to do it.

C: Not very beneficial and don't want to.

D: Not very beneficial but want to do it.

Give each option a score out of 10 or 100 (whatever works for you) for how much you want to take the action and again for how much it will benefit you. This will give you the co-ordinates for where that option sits on the graph. It is important that you are really honest here. Don't assume an action won't be beneficial just because you don't really want to do it. You can use this graph by plotting out all your options on it and see which area they fall into. Those that fall into area C (not very beneficial and don't really want to do it) can be eliminated right away. If these actions do not create a big enough benefit and you don't have the desire to do them, then there really isn't much point in considering them.

Remember when plotting your graph, everything is comparative. It is assumed that most, if not all of your options are beneficial. The score you give them depends on how beneficial they are when compared to the rest. Your least beneficial option, albeit very beneficial, will be in the lower half of the graph. An easier way to do this is by ranking your options in order then then giving them the correlating score. For example, if you have ten options, you rank them one to ten. The number one option gets ten points, the next nine points, then eight, then seven, and so on. Then you don't end up with many options having the same score. Although, if you really believe one option is just as beneficial as another, then give it the same score. It's really up to you, it's your model!

Now take a look at area D. These are the options you want to do but offer less benefit than others. You can eliminate these too - unless an option here was at the top of your want list, in which case, keep it to the side for now. Desire and reward are two powerful tools that can help to push you through when taking action. With enough desire, the reward does not need to be as big.

Next, have a look at the options in area A. These are the actions that have the most benefit but you don't really want to do them. Now it may be easy for you to disregard these as you don't really have much desire to do them, but before you do, take a moment to be really honest with yourself. One of these options may hold great benefit for you. It may even be the most beneficial of all! However, if you *really* don't wish to do it, then you shouldn't – and let's face it, you won't.

Lastly we have area B. These are the best options. These actions are both the most desirable *and* the most beneficial. With both traits combined, taking action will be easy *and* rewarding. Look at these options carefully. If your most desirable option fell into area D and most beneficial in area A, then include them in this list too. If your most desirable option *is* your most beneficial, then you have a winner. Don't concern yourself too much about making the 'right' decision. The good news is there is no 'wrong' decision. At this point, any of the actions would be beneficial to you and the making of your outcome.

The action you are looking for is the best one for you. Don't be fooled into thinking you have to pick just one either. In many cases, multiple actions can be taken and all the benefits attained. Each action moves you closer to where you want to be by bridging the gap. So this final part of selecting your action(s) is really just up to you.

Using the example from earlier, overleaf is the graph and list that may have been created so you can see the process:

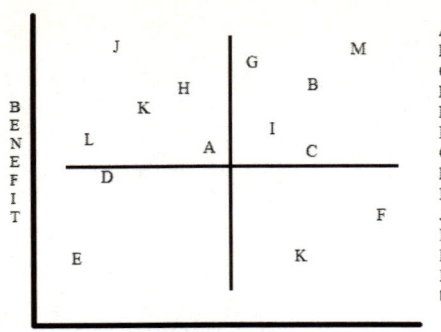

A: Bring in more people to help sell.
B: Get a business coach.
C: Provide samples of the product.
D: Invest in online advertising.
E: Research market preferences.
F: Create new innovative product.
G: Create pop up stand at local events.
H: Hand out leaflets.
I: Make special limited offers.
J: Bring in celebrity to market brand.
K: Host taster events.
L: Bring in a consultant/mentor.
M: Provide bulk options to large buyers.

HOW MUCH YOU WANT TO DO IT

Final action

Having made your final selection, you are now ready to start organising *when* you will take your action(s). Be specific with the day and time you will take it. Be honest with your expectation.

Think about the following:

- When will I take this action?
- How much time will I need?
- Will I take the whole action at once or break it up?
- What resources do I need?
- Who needs to know? Who else is involved? When will I tell them?

Resources

If to take this action all you need is yourself, some time, and energy, then you just need to make sure you have all three of these to get going. It is likely there are more resources you need to take your action. If your action involves going somewhere, then you will need a means of transportation. If you are making a purchase, then money or something to trade is required. Think about what resources you might need for your action. If there are any you need but do not currently have, then getting them becomes a priority outcome for you.

Team

Although this is *your* outcome, *you* who wants it, and overall *you* that is going to make it happen, remember that you are not alone in the endeavour. You can recruit a team that can support and assist you as you make your way through the process. There are a variety of different types of team members you could have.

Mentor: A mentor is someone who has already done what it is you are wanting to do or someone who possesses the qualities you wish to emulate in order to make your outcome happen. A mentor has the experience and wisdom that you can learn from in order to complete your project. Even if you never make contact with your mentor, having them as a role model is also beneficial. Observe their behaviours, attitudes, strategies, and processes. Find the key points and use them to improve your own actions.

Partner: This team member is someone who is looking to achieve the same outcome or something similar to yours. It can also be someone who is looking to go through a similar route to you, even though their final destination is different – like a body builder and a sprinter both going to the gym. Both training but for different things. Team up and use each other to motivate and drive one another to succeed. This is commonly found in gyms and in fitness circles, known as 'gym buddies'. When you hit the low moments – yes you will likely have them – or times that require that little extra push, having someone in your corner who really knows what you're going through to spur you on can make a huge difference. Your partner doesn't have to be local either. Take to the world wide web and find groups of people doing similar things. Start you own group if you like! Bounce ideas off each other and learn from one and other.

Friends: Friends are great for support and clarification. A friend who really believes in you and what you are doing is invaluable. It is useful to discuss your process with a friend and use them as a soundboard for your thoughts. They can view things from a different perspective and potentially point out blind spots or contribute ideas. A friend can be anyone who is willing to listen. A family member, a co-worker, or even someone you have just met. Every interaction holds the potential for learning.

Coach: A coach is a combination of these different types of team members. Someone who has the wisdom to guide, the understanding to push you, and the belief in your abilities. Working with a coach offers a great deal of learning to make your process simple and easy. With a coach you can progress faster and further than you would without one. They will also hold you accountable for following through with your plan.

One of the best parts of having a coach is having someone who is completely dedicated to you and your outcome. All the other team members are great and offer huge benefit, but they also have their own outcomes and obstacles to focus on, so their attention is limited. With a coach, *you* are the priority. You can talk all you want about you and what you are doing without that feeling of "Oh, I've been talking about myself this whole time. How selfish of me!". The coach wants to hear it all, and most of all, they actually *want* to help you.

The First Step

As the well-known quote says "You don't have to see the whole staircase, just take the first step." Using the 'Zoom method', you have a rough idea of what is ahead. The clearest and detailed part of the path is the part right in front of you. No matter how big the gap, how long the bridge, or how high it is, remember this:

You can only cross a bridge when you get to it.

Now your plan may be long, it may contain many steps, but the most important one right now is the first step. That first step in what is going to kick you off on this journey. Here's the thing, it is so easy to put things off (procrastinate) and so as a rule of thumb, your first action should be in the next twenty-four hours. It does not have to be a *huge* action with massive impact. Just do *something* that will take you a step closer to making your outcome happen. Plan it now and do it as soon as possible.

So the focus now is the first action you are going to take towards your first outcome. At this point nothing much else matters with regards to the plan. You have your big picture, you have your rough outline of the route, and now you have the launch pad. You have broken down the process so that you are clear on what it is you are going to do. Can you feel that tingle? That's you being ready.

Take some time to quickly review the plan. Think of anything you may have overlooked. As J.R.R. Tolhien wrote in The Hobbit, "It does not do to leave a live dragon out of your calculations if you live near him." This means taking everything into consideration when planning your immediate actions. Things can (and probably will) go wrong. This is covered more in stage five. As for now, you have your plan and that means you are a huge step closer to making it happen. On that note, I leave you with this quote:

"A goal without a plan is just a wish"

— Antoine de Saint-Exupéry

Some little reminders:

- The 'sweet spot' to planning is in the middle of detail and flexibility.
- The whole staircase is made up of many small steps.
- Your next step is the most important. The one in front of you.
- Know the result you want, not just the action you want to take.
- Explore your options. As many of them as you can.
- Use your resources (including your resourcefulness).
- Keep it clear, simple, and precise.

Five: Obstacles

"If you can find a path with no obstacles, it probably doesn't lead anywhere."

– Frank A. Clark

This tends to be the area that most people dread. It's the part that makes doing what we want so challenging. We try so hard to avoid them and yet they are always getting in the way. We see obstacles as the things that prevent us from getting where we want to be. They come in many forms and each is unique to the person in question.

By definition, an obstacle is something that obstructs or hinders progress. That may seem obvious but look carefully at what the definition means. An obstacle hinders and obstructs progress but it does *not* stop or prevent progress. By its very definition, an obstacle has to be overcome. If it is not overcome, then it was not an obstacle. Now you know ALL obstacles can be overcome, and they have to be.

Inevitable

It is important to realise what obstacles are and what they mean to you. If you are the kind of person who crumbles at the slightest speed bump, or runs away at the mere mention of risk or danger, then the journey of making what you want happen will be long and arduous. Don't worry though. Even if you are one of those people, it does not have to be that way.

First thing is to realise that obstacles can always be overcome. This you are already on your way to doing if you have not done so by now. The second is that obstacles are part of the process. They are not extras or things added on. They are actually there *for* you. Sounds crazy, I know. So let me explain.

We tend to only see the obstacles that get in our way when there is something we want. However, obstacles also get in the way of many things we *don't* want. We let these obstacles go unnoticed and take them for granted. You may be wondering what I'm talking about, so here are some examples:

- Your roof is an obstacle to the rain getting you and in your home.
- Your chair is an obstacle for gravity to stop you falling on the floor.
- Your coat is an obstacle to the cold getting to you.
- Your food is an obstacle to you getting hungry.
- Your sunglasses are an obstacle to the sun getting in your eyes.

These are very literal and physical examples of obstacles working for us. Obstacles can also be more psychological and emotional. For example, your friends and family are an obstacle to loneliness. Your job could be an obstacle to depression or poverty. We tend to not think about life without the things we already have, and what life would be like if we did not have them anymore. Now you have an idea of how obstacles work for you, take a moment to think about the useful obstacles in your life. Appreciate them and what they do for you. Be thankful and grateful. They are there *for* you, not against you. In a way, they are actually needed in order for things to happen the way they do. The key lesson here is this:

Obstacles make the way for things to happen the way they do.

So in order for us to make things happen, we must learn to work *with* obstacles, accept them as part of the process and use them to our advantage. Just as the mountains and hills do for the river. They lay the way for the water to flow in and around the land. The intention is never to stop the river or prevent it from reaching its final destination, only to guide it so that it may explore more of the land and itself. We can learn to manipulate obstacles so that when they appear, we *use* them. They go from being walls and fences, to being ladders and bridges, taking us further and higher than we could have gone without them.

Define

In order to use obstacles to our advantage, it is imperative to recognise them and define them clearly. Just as you did with your outcome, know it and know it well. Some obstacles can go unnoticed because they appear to have very little or no effect. You only notice them when it has got big enough to be a real problem. It is these types of obstacles that could potentially be slowing you down or preventing you from achieving more, faster. Ask yourself "Could I be doing any better?" If so, how? What is the reason that is stopping you? Once you are aware, you can choose whether to do something about it or not. Until you are aware, you cannot.

Other obstacles tend to be more obvious and they are easy to spot when we start out. The initial things that seem to be in our way to making the first moves. The 'gap' itself, between where you are and where you want to be can seem like an obstacle. We now know that this gap is actually the path to making it happen, not an obstacle.

When an obstacle presents itself, first of all don't panic. High emotion prevents logic. No logic makes it more difficult to process and problem solve. You know that the obstacle can be overcome, so you just need to figure out how. Start by defining clearly what the obstacle is and how exactly it is hindering your progress. The thing stopping you tends to be one of nine things. Super coach Michael Neill suggests they are:

- Time
- Fear
- Knowledge
- Money
- People
- Skill
- Energy
- Health
- Belief

When you are clear as to what the obstacle is, you can best tackle it. Some can appear to be obstacles at first but when you look carefully at them, you realise they are not. A client of mine had an important interview coming up at the end of the week when suddenly his car was hit and had to be taken in for repairs. He couldn't find a mechanic that could get the work done in time for the interview, and he began to panic. A couple of days passed and his panic only grew. "What will I do!? I'll never get the car fixed in time!" he exclaimed. He was so caught up in his perceived obstacle of the car being broken that he failed to define what the real obstacle was. The obstacle was actually that he needed a way of getting to the interview. "Do you really need the car for the interview?" I asked. Just like that, the doors opened, panic subsided, and he saw the light. "No!" he said with eyes wide open, looking up with a sense of amazing realisation. "I could get the train, or hire a car, a friend could take me, I could..." the options poured out.

Obstacles can be like clouds. They can cast shadows bigger than themselves and create darkness all around, but if you can see it for what it is and look past it, then all you will see is sunlight. Know your obstacles and know the question. Know the question and you will find the answer.

Failure

Just like obstacles, failure is something we try to avoid. Which makes sense after all, who wants to fail? The thing is – and you may be surprised to hear this, but – failure, just like obstacles, is part of the process. It is going to happen at some point and you must be ready for it. We can do our best to dodge failure when we see it coming. We can take precautions to minimise the risk of it. Despite the actions we take through anticipation, there are times that even against the odds, failure blindsides us and sweeps our feet from underneath you.

Although the event of failure is inevitable, the effect of it is very much within your control. You can let it defeat you, deter you from continuing, and give up. Or, like most of the most highly successful people in the world, you can learn from it. Each failure you experience has the potential to teach you a great lesson. With each lesson you can become better, stronger, more resilient, and wiser.

If you go through a whole process and never fail, then in some way you have failed yourself. You have not learnt or grown from the experience. Despite the success, you are just the same person you were when you started. Read any story of the greats and you will learn of their trials, errors, and mistakes. Some of the most legendary successes of history incurred failure after failure before they finally succeeded.

Michael Jordan once said "I've failed over and over and over again in my life, and that is why I succeed." Thomas Edison, when working on the lightbulb said "I have not failed. I have just found 10,000 ways that won't work." Bill Gates was quoted "It's fine to celebrate success but it is more important to heed the lessons of failure." These are just some examples of the attitude that allows failure to help you succeed, instead of derailing you from achievement.

Growing up, we are taught that failure is bad and that we must do what we can to avoid it at all costs. Failure is only bad if nothing is learnt. Then it is just a waste. It is only a negative event if it is allowed to stop you from moving forward. It is not a preventer of success, if anything it is one of the keys to it. Failure is feedback from reality and it lets us know that something needs to change. Find the lesson in failure, learn it and learn it well, grow from the experience, and you will succeed.

Even in the writing of this book, I experience a vital lesson through failure. My own preference was to write this book by hand as I just find it easier than typing. I had just finished stage three and my notepad was on the side by the window. A sudden storm came that evening. Somehow the rain had made its way onto the window ledge where my notepad sat. Although dry by the morning, the left side of all the pages had been left illegible.

Sure, I was angry, maybe even a little upset in that moment. But who was to blame? The weather for bringing rain? The notepad manufacturer for making it so absorbent? No, just me. My choice to hand write. My choice to leave the pad exposed to the elements. I had a think and realised that if this was so worth getting worked up over, then I should probably have taken better precautions. I continued to write by hand, and I re-wrote the first three stages. I also made sure that my notepad was kept safe and away from anything that could undo my work. Lesson learnt, life goes on.

Fear

Back in caveman times, fear was a useful tool for survival. The life of men and women back then was frequently under threat from the wild. The body's response to fear allowed for them to fight or escape, and live to see another day. Without the response of fear and its physiological effects, we would have perished. In fact, those who did not have the fearful ability probably did.

We still have this ability; however, we do not have as much of a need for it anymore. Life is considerably less dangerous nowadays. We don't have to worry about things like lions, sabretooth tigers, and other predators when we go outside. Yet we still very much experience fear from time to time. In the present, we fear things like loneliness, rejection, failure, loss, and embarrassment. However, none of these are actually things to be afraid of. You cannot physically fight rejection. You can't run from loss. You can only fight them mentally because that is where they are, in your head.

We used to fear things that could end our lives and now we fear things that can lead to us *feeling* like our life is over, with such negative feelings that cause us emotional pain. Yet nothing can *make* you feel these things, only what you think about them can. Most modern day fears are not of what is actually happening, they are in fact of what we think is going to happen in the future. They are all made from assumptions.

Accept that you do not know the future. Accept that even if the thing you fear - such as rejection or failure - does happen, you will be ok. You will survive. Fear is there to let you know you must be conscious of the moment right now. Be here and now so you can be at your best. Get your mind out of the fearful future you perceive. The present requires your attention so you can act in such a way that takes what you want the future to be, and make it happen.

You

The obstacles that have been mentioned so far have merely been a lack of resource or opportunity, or some kind of negative experience. They can all be overcome by gaining whatever is missing. Finding a way to fill that gap or jump over it. If you do that, then there is no issue. However, there is one obstacle to overcome, the most challenging, the most common, and yet the one that everyone should tackle first.

The only real obstacle to making it happen is YOU.

Right now you are either subtly shaking your head in disbelief, thinking "What!? No I'm not! I'm the one *making* it happen!" Or you are gently nodding, thinking "That's right, I do tend to get in my own way when it comes to getting what I want." Either way, it must be accepted. Once you have accepted it, you can now *do* something about it.

As I said before, most obstacles are just an absence of opportunity or resource. The obstacle to that resource is –wait for it… drumroll– is you. Or better yet, the *way* to that resource is you. As Tony Robbins once said to me – and a thousand other people at one of his 'Unleash the Power Within' events – "The best resource you can have is resourcefulness." It's true, it really is. Think about it. If you can be resourceful enough then anything you need or want so you can move forward, you can get and do so.

Take a moment to think about how you may be being an obstacle to your own project. Is there an area that you may be being narrow minded in and missing a great opportunity? Is there an action you are avoiding because you fear taking it or won't energise yourself enough to do it? Perhaps you refuse to ask for help because your pride stands in the way to protect your ego – believe me, I know what that's like. Maybe you have convinced yourself you don't deserve the opportunity and so it is not even worth trying.

All of these obstacles are evident through you. They are not always easy to see, though. We naturally don't like being in the wrong and we definitely don't like being blamed. This is not about pointing the finger and saying whose fault it is. This is about taking responsibility for your own progress and working on any hindrance to it, including yourself! Be honest – not critical or berating, just honest – with what you see when you take a close look at what *you* are doing (or not doing) to make this project go better, faster, further. You don't even have to change anything if you don't want to. You just need to be aware of what is happening.

Attitude

When it comes down to it, the magnitude of any obstacle is really dictated by your perception and attitude towards it. The reality you experience is filtered by the thoughts and feelings you have about it. If you think life is hard, then the chances are it will feel hard. If you believe life is a gift and you are lucky to have the opportunity to experience it, then you are in for a better ride than the former.

The same applies to how you look at obstacles. We now know they are inevitable and part of the process. So the question is how are you going to react when the next one presents itself? How are you going to view it? What are you going to be saying to yourself? There is a direct correlation between your attitude towards an obstacle and the perceived difficulty of overcoming it. This is demonstrated in the graph below.

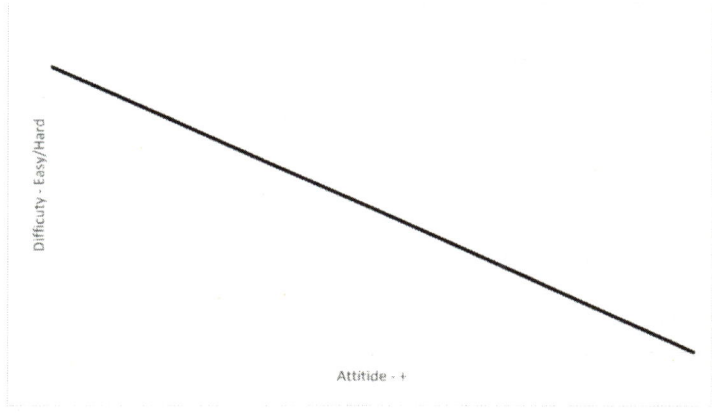

This concept may seem really simple, and that is because it is. If your attitude towards the obstacle is very negative, then that obstacle is going to be more of a challenge than if you were to have a more positive one. The obstacle itself does not change, just the light you view it in. You may have heard the phrase 'To make a mountain out of a molehill'. Well your attitude has the power to make molehills out of mountains too. Your perception is everything, and the good news is that your perception is up to you.

The process is simple, but that does not mean easy. The way you see the obstacle – or more specifically, the way you think about the obstacle – effects the way you feel. The way you feel effects the way you behave, and the action you take. What you do dictates the results you get i.e. overcoming the obstacle or not.

Dwell

Another factor that contributes to your perception of an obstacle is the time you spend thinking about it and not doing anything about it. The more pessimistic of those among us are able to find the negatives, the worst parts of any hindrance to progress. Given enough time, these obstacles are made bigger and insurmountable. Potential fatalities become so called truths and then nothing else seems possible in the mind of the beholder.

When an obstacle does present itself, don't ignore it or sit on it. It will grow if left untamed. Face it right away knowing it can be overcome. Define it, make your plan, and set out your intention. Get the gears moving immediately. Avoid dwelling on it and thinking of ways it could stop you. Focus your mind on the climb. How will this obstacle be just another step forward? Use the momentum you have built already and continue strong without delay.

Pause

There are times when obstacles will catch us by surprise. In fact, most obstacles are unexpected. When they do pop up out of nowhere, don't panic. It can be an impulse to react in a non-constructive way. Things like yelling, crying, hitting things, and sulking, none of these will change what is happening. They are just forms for dwelling and resistance. They might make you feel a little better but this feeling is short lived. Do not stay here. Move forward. Staying in a negative state, acting in unnecessary ways, it can only make things worse. Instead, take a time out. Breathe. Take a few deep breaths. Count them. One… Two… Three… In… and out. Then ask yourself the almighty question of moving forward.

"Now what?"

As if you were being asked by your best friend. Listen to your intuition and start adapting your plan. Solutions are everywhere. The problem is always solvable and you know your life best to solve it. Act with logic and reason to create a way of acting that allows you to continue progressing. So what something went wrong. So what, you missed an opportunity. So what it didn't go the way you planned. Now what? Don't stop moving forward. Speed bumps are made to go over them. That's all this is. Duck and move. Bob and weave. Float like a butterfly and...

You know the rest. Getting knocked back does not mean knocked out. Sometime life hits you hard, and when it does, that is when you need to start hitting back.

You don't have to be positive *all* the time. It is natural for things like doubt, disbelief, thoughts of giving up, and excuses to stop, crossing your mind. Don't feel bad when they do. Even the most successful people in the world have them. Acknowledge them and accept them for what they are. Just thoughts. Once you have done that, you can make a choice of how to act moving forward. You can hold on to the thought and let it weigh you down by resisting or overthink on it, or you can let it pass, put it down, and take action to continue on your way to making things happen.

Patience

Or more precisely, impatience. Making things happen – especially big things – can take time. It is understandable to feel like things are taking forever. When this happens, just check in with yourself and look at what you are doing. Are you doing everything you can? Is there a way to speed things up? Or are things actually just taking as long as they should but you're being impatient about it?

The bigger the outcome, the more that needs to be put in. Without time, nothing can happen. This is why enjoying the journey is so vital. You have to be passionate and enthusiastic about what you do because if you're not, then it feels hard. Time will drag on and motivation dissipates. But if you're driven and committed then you will always find something to *do* to help move you forward, and in doing so time will fly. Having won the event before is great, but it's nothing compared to the time of winning it; and winning it starts now. Hang in there.

Ready

Now you are becoming the person you need to be to get things done. You are ready to face whatever comes your way. Not only will you be able to handle any kind of adversity that stands before you, you may even be looking forward to when they reveal themselves, as you know how each one holds the potential for learning and growth.

With your new found attitude and perception, you do not fear challenge, you expect it. You anticipate the hard bits. They don't make you unhappy. If anything, you approach each one with a smile knowing the opportunity for progress awaits you. You can now face adversity head on and hold out a hand of acceptance because you know that it has come to help guide you, not stop you.

In the end you will stand high on the rubble of broken obstacles. With each one you conquer, you are left standing higher and higher. It is because you came this way that future obstacles appear smaller, inferior to the level you have reached. Others will look up to you and marvel, asking "how did you do it?" You can them help them so that they may stand high with you. There is no limit to how high you can go, only the limits of your own imagination and determination.

Now you are ready to walk the path you have laid out before you. In the next stage we are going to add some fuel to the fire that burns within you so you can rocket your way to where you want to be. When you choose to, turn the page and meet me where we will get you pumped with motivation. Even more than you already are!

Remember:

- Obstacles are inevitable and part of the process.
- They do not stop you. They guide you.
- Know your obstacle and it can be overcome.
- Failure and fear can work *for* you, if you let them.
- YOU are the biggest obstacle to what you want.
- Your attitude dictates the size of an obstacle.
- Don't dwell on it. Breathe and move forward.

Six: Motivation

"Wake up determined. Go to bed satisfied."

— Dwayne 'The Rock' Johnson

Motivation is something that everybody wants and yet so many seem to lack. Some people have never really thought about what it is or how to get it when they want some. To them, it is some kind of rare illusive concept that in any given moment, they either have it or they don't. It is not a tangible thing that you can pick up or collect. It is an *internal* process that you go through before taking action.

For any action to happen, it requires motivation. It is the energy that initiates and guides the behaviour towards a goal or outcome. You experience highs and lows of it every single day. Have you ever taken time to look at the moments where you are most motivated? If you do, then you can create a bank of resources to use in times where motivation may be dipping.

When we want to do something, we do it. Providing there is the opportunity, resource, permission, and it is ethical. We naturally desire immediate gratification, so the actions we know will bring a more instant reward tend to be more motivating. For example, when we are hungry – I mean *really* hungry – then we desire something to satisfy us as soon as possible. Rather than think carefully about what to eat and making good choices, we just think "I've got to eat *something*." With less regard to what exactly. The lesson here is:

If you wait until you a starving, you will eat ANYTHING, even if it is bad for you.

This applies to more than just food. If you are broke, you will do more to get money (cheat, steal, borrow). If you are alone, you will settle for anyone. If you are unhappy, you will do anything to change this feeling or even numb it (e.g. sex, drugs, and alcohol). Your focus becomes the more urgent outcome and its importance means you are willing to do whatever it takes to make it happen instantly. This can be a great motivator when set up well, but more often it happens when unplanned. In these situations, it is better to refer to the original outcome such as 'eating well' and taking action to *prevent* a similar situation happening in future.

Our basic needs according to Abraham Maslow (a renowned psychologist known for his creation of the Hierarchy of Needs in 1943) are food, sex, breathing, and homeostasis[1].

All of these are great motivators for action, and when one is lacking, we tend to make it a priority over anything else, and we are willing to take drastic measures to get it. As Eric Thomas says "When you want to succeed as bad as you want to breathe, then you will be successful." That may sound a little extreme but the key point is true. If you were deprived of air or food or water, what would you be willing to do to get it? When you feel you *need* something, you will do what it takes. You will be motivated.

---

[1] Homeostasis: The regulation of conditions in the body such as CO_2 levels, temperature, and water content. Our internal environment. Our nervous system and hormones regulate this. Isn't the body amazing!?

Now perhaps the outcome you are working towards is not a necessity. Regardless, you do still really, really want it and that is enough. When we really, deeply, truly want something with all our mind, body, and soul, then we will do what it takes. When our motivation is tested, it is simply a question of:

How much do you want it?

Once you have answered that question truthfully, then the question is what are you going to *do* about it? Motivation is ever changing. It can stay high or stay low, but even then it is not consistent through time. The thing to remember is that you are *ALWAYS* motivated. Believe it or not, it's true. Think about it. Whatever you are doing at any moment, you are motivated to do it. Even if it is rest, sleep, watch tv, something is motivating you to do so. You may not be aware of it but there is something, some kind of desire or reason that is motivating you to do it.

Procrastination may seem like a time where you are not motivated enough to do something but it is actually that you are *more* motivated to do something else. Again, this comes back to instant gratification.

You may want to finish that project for work so you can impress your boss and potentially get that promotion, but that will require time and energy. You also want to sleep and relax. This can be achieved right now and so it is more appealing and thus a lot more motivating."

Stop Procrastination

To shift the motivation, all you have to do is shift your focus. Instead of thinking about deciding between working on the project or sleep (because sleep will win, especially if your bed is right there and looks really comfy), think about the outcomes and meanings of each. The choice then becomes sleep or get promoted. If you want that promotion enough, then you will be motivated to get that project done. If you don't really want it that much, or want to go to bed more because getting enough sleep is more beneficial, then fine, go to bed. The choice and responsibility are all yours. The important thing is that you consciously make the decision knowing full well what it is you are choosing.

Being motivated or having motivation is merely a state of mind in the present moment. Your mindset is made up of what you desire, what you focus on, and what you need to do to make it happen. This simple formula is one to keep in mind:

Desire + Action x Focus = Motivation

Notice how focus is a multiplier, not just an addition. This is because you can have a whole lot of desire and will to act, but if your mind is not focused on them, it will have a large impact on your motivation. Focus can also be a negative. If your focus is on the work required in the action and your perception of this is negative, then this will dramatically decrease your level of motivation. Ideally you have a high level of desire, a high level of will to act, and a high degree of focus on a positively assumed outcome. Then your motivation will be high. If you feel your motivation is lacking, have a think about which part of the formula may need a boost.

Taking control

It may seem like your state of mind and feelings are beyond your control but I assure you, they are not. Emotion is a by-product of our thoughts. They allow us to express ourselves and connect with others. Those cavemen and women who expressed emotion probably connected with others better and were able to form relationships that aided their survival, and so this ability has grown through evolution. We are naturally emotional beings. However, in most cases, we merely feel the way we think we should at any given moment. If something we label as 'sad' happens, then it would be expected to display a sad emotion and considered unusual if you didn't. It is almost like an instinctive reaction. This is not always obvious, especially when *in* a highly emotional state. Don't worry though, this impulsive reaction can be processed and trained.

Rather than looking at what has happened and believing it was some kind of external event that made you feel this way, stop for a moment. Take a breath, and look inward at what you are thinking about what has happened. Then think what the typical or expected emotional reaction would be. Chances are, that is what you are feeling. If you think you have been wronged somehow, you could expect to be angry, but do you *have to* be angry? Something to ponder over is 'What would it *mean* if you didn't feel that way?' Your answer will either be your motivation to be angry, or a realisation that you don't have to be.

It is a simple process of Thought > Feeling > Behaviour, just as we have discussed before. So when it comes to motivation, the thoughts you have will set the stage for the feeling of motivation to enter so that your action (behaviour) can be performed. Motivation is a precious thing and there are many different types. There are many ways to motivate and inspire yourself. Here are just a few examples.

Music

Popular among athletes, music is a great way to evoke a state or emotional response in people. It has the ability to focus the mind, facilitate mental imagery, manipulate brain wave frequencies, and recall association. That may all sound a little complex, but it is all on a subconscious level, so you don't have to think too much about it. Just listen and feel.

Different songs have different effects on different people. To you, a particular piece of music may help you to feel strong and powerful, but to another, cautious and fearful. Our minds are unique and the way we process is too. Everyone has a type of music or a particular song that generates a feeling of 'Let's go!'. For me it is *Proud* by Heather Small. One of many that I have collected over the years. Find yours and create a playlist of motivation. Then whenever you need a boost, get on the headphones and hit play.

Speeches

Just like music, speeches have the power to inspire. As oppose to tune and melody, speeches speak directly to us through language. Motivation speeches can spark fires within us and charge us up for massive action. The speech doesn't even have to be anything to do with what you are doing, as the general theme is 'You can do it!'.

YouTube is a great place for this, along with many other video providers online. Les Brown is a great motivation speaker who can really boost you to go for your dreams and make it all the way. I credit him with a large amount of my own motivation over the years. There has been a plethora of inspiring speeches made over time. Find the ones that resonate with you and keep them handy. Just like the music, get on the headphones and hit play whenever you need.

Text

Sometimes the spoken word is not always available, but fortunately inspiring words have been collected through history and written down. Turn to the books of great thought leaders who have been known to completely change the world and the way it works. I recommend the great philosophers of all time such as Seneca, Marcus Aurelius, Socrates, Plato, and Aristotle.

Motivation can even come from a single sentence. Quotes can be found in their thousands online. Find the ones that really hit home for you and make a note of them. I like to write them on a sticky note and put them on the wall by my desk – which doesn't really have much wall left – so I can be inspired by them every day. They are quick and easy to refer to, and yet their effect can be huge on your state of mind. Motivating through inspiration.

For those who like poetry, check out *If* by Rudyard Kipling. One of my personal favourites. Michael Caine does a fantastic reading which can be found on the web.

Stories

As with speeches and text, stories use language to take us on a journey. Stories of other people's fights with adversity, overcoming of dire obstacles, and achieving great successes, they all have the ability to lift us up and fling us towards action. These stories can be fiction and still move us in a way that leads us to move forward. The pictures they paint ignite our imagination to think in a way that says 'Yes, I can' and 'I will.'

Documentaries are a good way to see what others have done and what they went through to do it. Their strength and persistence becomes our own. Like heat from a fire, the energy transfers to us and builds. We make empowering comparisons and think yes! If they can climb Mount Everest with no food, little water, and wearing shorts - Wim Hof, search for him, you'll be amazed – then I can give this presentation at work, get up and go to the gym, go talk to that attractive person, or whatever it is you want to do. It can really give you some perspective when you see what is possible. Most of all, stories can teach us lessons about what can be done, what we can do, and to go for it.

Role Model

If you have selected a role model for your journey, then turn to them for inspiration. Remember, your role model does not have to be someone who has done or is doing what you want to do. They just need to have some kind of attribute that you wish to emulate. A quality that you would like to see in yourself. Be it their courage, their unique way of thinking, or just how they conduct themselves in public; Look at them and what they have done. Allow their actions to guide you forward and ignite your own actions.

As well as having someone to look up to, think of how others can look up to you. Imagine *you* are somebody's role model and your life is an example to guide them. What kind of example do you want to set? Show them how it is done. Take responsibility for being a role model to anyone that has ever wanted to make something happen. Let the responsibility motivate you to act in such a way that drives you forward as the kind of person you want to be.

Memory

You are always motivated. In your life there are going to be times where you were more motivated than others. These memories are also a source of motivation. You can think back to the moments when you felt your highest peaks of motivational energy. The times where you were so motivated and determined that you felt unstoppable. You can also think back to the great successes of your past. The times where you got what you wanted, made something happen, defeated the odds, and came out on top.

Either way, you can think back to one of those times and relive the experience. Take a moment to sit comfortably, somewhere you can be at peace. Close your eyes and cast your mind back. Build up the memory in your mind. Think about what you can see, what you can hear, and what you can feel. What are you saying to yourself? Who else is there? What are they saying? Really go for the details. Where you are, what's around, what's the temperature like? Create a vivid image for you to step into. Don't worry if there are parts you can't remember. Fill in the gaps with things that will empower you. If you can't remember what people were saying, just assume it was something like "Wow, you're amazing!" or "You're a legend!" (my personal fave). Recreate those feelings that you had and bring them into the now to motivate you in this moment.

Your Why

One of the biggest sources of motivation is your 'Why'. Looking back at stage three, you should have created a powerful reason for doing what you are doing. If you have made this reason big enough, bigger than you, then it will push you through at all times. Anything that comes up against you, your why must be bigger. When life hits you in the face, your why has to hit back harder.

Even if you are moving forward solely on the why of 'I just want it', then you have to want it more than anything that tries to obstruct you. You have to want it more than you want to stop, and there *will* be times where you want to stop. It's ok to pause. There's only so much you can – and should – do in a day. It is a battle of desire. No matter what happens, it will be what you want. Always do what you want, but be aware of wanting it. If you stop, it is because you want to, for whatever reason. Be it you just don't want to continue, or you believe you cannot go on, if you stop, the wanting of stopping is there. If you never want to stop, you won't.

Remember the intension you are setting out with. Recall the reason you are doing this. WRITE IT DOWN. If you can, make it as short as possible. One sentence or even a single word. The *reason* does not need to be small. This is just something short to remind you of it. The easier it is for your mind to access it, the better it will drive you through the challenges. Make you reason your mantra. Repeat it to yourself when you need that little bit extra to get you to keep moving forward.

**As simple as they are, the words
'I can' hold great strength.**

Success

Yep, that's right. Success is a motivator. Who would have thought!? When we succeed, we are motivated to keep being successful. The good news is we can use this to our advantage when making things happen. Success can come from anywhere. You do not have to succeed at what you are working on in order to get the motivational benefits. You can take on any task that you will be successful at, and it can contribute to the motivation you have for working on the project. This is how having to-do lists can help to create momentum. Remember, little successes build to create big ones.

In the moments where the task at hand seems daunting and you can't really be bothered because you think it will be a lot of work, take on some smaller tasks (related or not), and get some success under your belt. Take on tasks that you know are easy and won't take long. Successful people are successful because they succeed, not the other way around. Be it running little errands like taking out the trash, or helping someone else with what they are working on, a little success goes a long way. WARNING: Success can be addictive and these kinds of tasks can end up being used as a way of procrastinating or avoiding the original task. Set your list and stick to it. Use them as a tool *for* your outcome, not *against* it.

Expectation

In times of hardship, our motivation can dwindle. Although it is rarely because of the events of the present moment, but more due to our thoughts of the potential future as a result. If you lose your job, then it is easy to imagine that this will lead to you going bankrupt, losing your home, being homeless, starving, alone. Drastic, I know, but this is how some people's minds work. They enter this downward spiral with no real evidence, just their own perception.

When your outlook is bleak, your motivation can follow. Your focus is a multiplier, remember? Even if now seems tough, you don't *know* it is going to stay that way unless you act in a way that *makes it* stay that way. To *do* anything about it requires motivation, so do yourself a favour and shift your focus. Start thinking best case scenario. You can still be realistic, but be open to positive possibilities too. A swift change in perspective can work wonders. Working with a coach is great if this is something you struggle with.

If you lose your job, then you gain time. You are now free to do something else. Something potentially better. The times that can seem like the worst of your life can actually end up being the best thing that ever happened to you. That's up to you. This is your story, you are the author, and you decide how it ends. If you fall, you get back up. If you get knocked back, you push forward. If you fail, you learn. If you lose, you grow. If something tries to stop you, you either move around it or you go straight through it. There is always a way. Always.

A constant reminder I use is whatever way I go… **GO ALL THE WAY.**

Motivation is a precious thing and there are many different types. The best motivation comes from within, as you always have it with you. There are many other types that you can get from the world around you, many of which we have already discussed. Finding what motivates you isn't always easy but it is worth looking for. A coach can help to point out the motivators you may be missing or just have not noticed. They can also be a source of motivation themselves as they want you to progress and can encourage you to do so.

Pumped

Now you are pumped and ready to take on the world, take on life. You have built yourself an arsenal of motivators, you are aware of the blocks and disrupters to your inner energy, and you see the outcome you want to make happen. Can you feel it?

That sense of power to do anything! Congratulations on coming this far. You are part of the small percentage of people who are taking control of their lives and making things happen.

You have come a very long way on this journey. I commend you for sticking it out. Clearly you are serious about this outcome and it is becoming an inevitability. That is awesome! We are nearing the final stages now. It is time to take everything you have learned so far, and put it into practice. Join me in the next stage where the real action happens.

So when it comes to getting motivated, remember:

- Action is easy when you have no other viable options.
- If you really want it, you'll do what it takes.
- Stay focused.
- Inspiration can be found anywhere. Motivation is found within.
- Know your 'why'.
- GO ALL THE WAY

Seven: Action

"The path to success is to take massive, determined actions."

– Tony Robbins

This is it. You have now reached a major stage of your journey. Now is where everything comes together to create real change. With regards to making it happen, everything up to this point has been the 'making' and now is where 'it happens'. This is where theory becomes practical. The seeds have been sewn and it is now time to start reaping. For some, action can be the most challenging step. It is easy to talk about what you are going to do; it is another to actually do it. The difficulties come from being ill-prepared, of which you are not. If you have taken the time and put in the energy into each stage leading up to this point, then this stage will actually be relatively easy.

When you have a clear objective you want to achieve, an important reason why, a well-planned strategy, a strong attitude to adversity, and the motivation to always move forward, then making it happen is a lot easier than it would be if you did not. All of your learnings and preparation will pay off most in this stage. You already know most of the answers to any questions that may come up. Key things such as what you are going to do, when you are going to do it, where, and how. These have all been covered in your planning. Now we are going to go through some ways to make the 'action' part even easier. Right from knowing what to do, to actually doing it.

Make it easy

Sometimes there are things we do not really want to do but we want the outcome that doing it will bring. Your mind is focused on the result and this motivates you to do it, but still, actually doing it is a drag. This can be changed by altering the nature of the task and by making it more convenient.

If you are planning to go to the gym three times a week but the thought of getting up early, getting ready, and having to make the journey to the gym leaves you feeling reluctant, then make it easy. Prep as much as you can the day before. Pre-mix an energy shake so it is waiting for you when you wake up. Pack your bag and lay out your gym clothes. Make the process smooth and simple so that all you have to do is wake up and go. You will form habits and routines. Soon you will be able to do this on autopilot. It will feel so easy.

When working on a project, give yourself a good space to work in. Remove possible distractions that can hold you back from being productive. If you allow them the chance to distract you then they will. Set up a block of time where nothing else matters and you can then focus solely on the task at hand. Even if you do not get much done, just set it up. Make it hard *not* to do what you want to do, then it becomes easy.

It's hard NOT to work out when you've already made the effort to get to the gym.

Sometimes the current situation makes it a challenge to get motivation or into the 'right frame of mind', but the real challenge is for you to *create* the situation where you operate at your best. You think a surgical room is just set up for sanitisation? No, it's also set up in a way that allows the surgeon to just focus on the operation they are performing. You can do the same. Decide what environment you want to be in so you can function to the highest degree. Open space or closed off? Alone or with others? Music, ambient noise, or silence? Discover the variables that work *for* you, and remove those that obstruct your excellence. For me, during the writing of this book, I found I could get a lot more writing done when sat comfortably reclined on the sofa with acoustic guitar and piano playing in the background. Whereas before I would make myself sit at my desk and listen to classical music. Now I find it a lot easier to write for longer periods of time because I feel more at ease and in the flow. It is up to you to *make* this happen, not just wait and hope for it to happen on its own.

Break it down

Some tasks can seem big and a little daunting. When it comes to acting on them, you can make it easier by breaking it down into small chunks. When writing this book, I set myself the task of writing at least three pages a day. Although, even that sometimes seemed like a lot, and even in my own personalised work environment, it was a struggle. So instead I would say, "Fine, today I will just write a paragraph". This task was a lot easier, and I knew full well that if I could get a single paragraph done then a few pages was naturally going to come out with it. But even if they didn't, that was ok.

Achieving an average amount may seem…well, average. However, if you can achieve an average amount consistently over a long enough time line, it can actually build up to be great things. Take saving money for example. You want to go on holiday to the other side of the world next summer, and it will cost you around £2500. That may seem like too much money. Let's say the trip is eleven months away. That is forty-four weeks. So if you can put aside just £35 a week, you could be on your way next year. That is just £5 a day! Suddenly, that large amount of cash is not so big and your dream holiday is very much within reach. £5 a day; What does that mean to you? A sandwich and drink? A train fare? A drink on a night out? Or could it mean sipping Mai Tai on a beautiful beach watching the sunset?

With a long enough timeline and consistent action, you can get anywhere. You can *do* anything. Consistency is key. Get into the habit of progressing. Even if just a little bit, make a step forward EVERY SINGLE DAY. You don't always have to move in leaps and bounds, but consistent advancement sets you up for when they happen. You avoid the risk of blocks or falling into ruts because your success is ever growing and you are ever moving forwards.

Remember that success breeds success. When you act productively, you stimulate yourself to continue. You can break down your task into smaller steps and focus on just completing that first one, and you have made that first step so easy that there is no reason you can't take it. With that little success you are now a little more pumped for step two, and the process continues. Sometimes the tasks don't even have to be related. Make a to-do list and work your way through it. Chuck some really easy ones that won't take long. With each one you cross off, you gain momentum and getting through them gets easier. Have you ever had one of those day where you have something to do early in the morning or you start the day with a productive task like clearing up, and then you feel the urge to continue the productivity throughout the day? The opposite can also happen. Spend the morning doing nothing and then doing *anything* feels like a huge effort.

Each step takes you higher, closer to the next. Your steps make the climb to success a staircase instead of a mountain side.

You can also do the complete opposite and shorten your to-do list to just one key thing you plan to do. Write it down and show yourself how nothing else needs to be done other than this one task. Or maybe you make it so that nothing else *can* be done until it is complete. I once had a client who wanted to change their eating habits. They had tried a wide variety of diets and eating methods, but they always ended up snacking and over-eating. "It's too hard", they said. "So what if you made it easy?" I replied. It's not that eating well was hard, it was that snacking and over-eating was so easy. His house was full of snacks and quick to make processed foods. He would spend around £80 a week on food just for himself.

So we did some research on healthier foods that he liked and I accompanied him on his next food shop. Now the food he bought wasn't all greens and meats, but it was free of snacks and 'quick foods'. A month later we spoke, he told me how much better he was feeling. He had lost 8lbs and saved over £160. I asked him what was different to the diets he had done before. He said "The diets before were not tasty. I would get hungry and end up grabbing a snack. Those snacks would turn into binge meals and I'd eat too much. But now I feel full after a meal. Plus, even if I wanted to snack, there aren't any. So I'd have to go all the way to the shop just to get some. That was more effort than it was worth."

He got results by making what he wanted easy, and making what he didn't want, hard. Not having snacks within reach in his house made it easy not to gorge whenever he was peckish. Think about the change you want to make. How could you make what you want to do easier and make it harder not to? This is another way of creating your environment. Find what works best for you.

When you break down a task, you see it more clearly and in more detail. Just as we did with the Zoom Method. The better you know exactly what needs to be done, the easier you can make it for yourself. It may not even be something that you need to do yourself. It's just something that needs to be done. Delegate if you wish, and save yourself time. Prioritise your time and energy as you only have a certain amount each day. Choose carefully how you distribute it, and you will be rewarded appropriately.

Reward

You may have heard of the use of the 'carrot and the stick' when it comes to motivation. As humans, we tend to be attracted to things that reward us (the carrot), and avoid those that lead to punishment (the stick). You can use this to your advantage by setting up a system that rewards you for doing your 'to-dos' or gives you 'the stick' if you don't. For example, you could treat yourself to a trip or experience as a reward for completing a task, or not allow yourself to have something you would normally have because you didn't.

This requires motivation and a strong will as it is really easy to just reward yourself for nothing, just because you feel like it. Some people also make the error of rewarding themselves *before* the task, and then they end up not doing it. They say "I'll treat myself to this and *then* I will do the work." This is effective for those with the will to commit to the action, but once you have had the reward, the incentive to do the work is not as strong.

A way to get around this is to make the control external. Bring someone else in to be in charge of the reward and punishment allocating. A young lady I worked with used this method when training for a marathon. She gave her best friend £400 and said "If I don't run an extra mile every week for twelve weeks, you can donate this." Now her reward was the money if she completed the task, but more so her punishment for not doing it would be that she lost it. If you're wondering what happened, she completed the task, and the marathon, and then gave half the money to charity and used the other half for a rewarding spa weekend with her friend. Everyone's a winner.

We are naturally drawn towards or away from things. This is what keeps us moving. Set up systems that move you. Having a coach is great for this as it creates an external form of accountability and helps you to explore different systems available. Be it by moving towards a reward or away from a punishment, the carrots and sticks you place in your world will make it easier for you to take action and keep on going every day on your way to making things happen.

Rehearse

When an action is important or we only have one opportunity to do it, we can improve our chances of success through rehearsal. Take some time to think it though and imagine how it is going to go, the best way it can. Imagine the scene; Where you are, who's there, what you are wearing, what you are saying, as much detail as you can. If this makes you feel nervous, then I recommend doing it often. Remember that right here and now is safe. You are not in any danger. You are free to think about it. After enough times, you will get so used to the situation that when it comes to doing it, you will be more than ready.

Mental rehearsal also allows you to plan for different variables such as peoples responses, the weather, or transport issues. The world can be unpredictable at times, but the more you are prepared for, the more things will go your way because your way is every way. No limits, no surprises. Whatever comes, you can handle it. In your mind, you have already handled it. So much stress comes from thinking we can't handle the current situation. The more prepared you are, the more you realise that you *can* handle it, and so there is no stress.

Our minds are powerful things. We can imagine events so vividly that our bodies feel it as if it may be happening as we think it. You may notice that when you imagine something sad, your breathing becomes deep, your eyes may begin to water, or nose starts to run. If you picture a bad experience where you were angry, your shoulders and jaw may tense up, heart rate increases, and perhaps you begin to sweat. Nothing is actually happening to you right now to cause these effects, but your body reacts as if it was. Your body takes your thoughts and makes them real.

By being well prepared, you allow yourself to be able to act proactively and create the results you want by guiding the present there. Without preparation, you force yourself into a situation where all you can do is react to the results of actions made by people other than yourself. Being proactive means taking responsibility for outcomes a taking action first. It means not waiting till you have to or till you have no choice.

You have a choice. Make it.

Decide. Commit:

You have your desired outcome and your plan to make it happen. You have prepared for obstacles and you have your reasons. Now let me ask you this: Have you made the decision?

Everything changes when you make a choice to take an action and commit to it. When you decide that this is it. That you are really going to do this. You are going to go for it with everything you got. You write it down, you talk about it, but most of all you believe right down to your core that "This is what I'm going to do" and you do it.

A decision this strong is like making a promise to yourself. You shouldn't make promises you can't keep, and you shouldn't make decisions you won't meet. What is a decision with no follow up of action? It is just words. Words of mild intention but may as well be ignored. Are you someone to be ignored? When you make a promise, does it mean anything? Look yourself in the eye or just look forward and envision yourself doing what you want to do. Say what you are going to do. Say it with conviction. "I want this. I'm making it happen."

When you make a commitment – I mean a *real* commitment – to doing something, you'll be amazed at what you will do to get it done. Think of a time where you had a task of utmost importance. That task inevitably had obstacles but they didn't matter because you had committed to getting it done. Commitment is the ultimate weapon against failure. As the saying goes "He who never gives up, never fails." Like a child learning to walk. They will fall many, many times.

However, they are committed to walking like those around them, and they will not stop trying until they do.

There are various ways to enforce your own commitment. You can make a promise to yourself. Take a minute to create your promise. Make it clear what you are going to do. Then stand in front of a mirror (or somewhere you can clearly see your reflection), look yourself dead in the eye, and repeat your promise three, four, or even five times. To really cement it into your subconscious, repeat the promise, but each time put emphasis on a different word. If your promise has seven words, then you will overall say it seven times.

A simple example:

I can do it.
I **can** do it.
I can **do** it.
I can do **it**.

Another way to reinforce your commitment is to tell people about what you are doing. The more people you tell, the more committed you will be. The more times you talk about it, the more it will be imbedded into your subconscious (so be warned, only do this is you really are going to commit!). Say what it is you are going to do, tell the world, and do it. By having people know, you are likely to be asked about it in future. This will enforce your action as there is now more of an expectation, as well as your own. There is a social responsibility to get it done now that people know. You have made the action bigger than just you.

When you do tell people, avoid stating an intention like "I'm going to…" Saying that you are 'going to' is another form of procrastination. Unless an action can only be done at a certain time in the future, then there is no reason you can't start right now. If you are quitting smoking, then don't tell people you are 'going to' quit smoking. This delays action. You now have the opportunity to put it off indefinitely. Instead, tell them that you *have* quit smoking. Now the onus is on you to follow up that statement with action, and if anyone sees you smoking they will say "Hey, I thought you quit!", whereas if you just stated the intension rather than the commitment, they would just assume you have not started yet, or that you changed your mind. Rather than trying and failing, you just failed to even try.

Discipline

As I've said before, this outcome is yours and it is up to you. No one wants it more and no one is going to do more than you to make it happen. So in doing so, it is very important that you are disciplined with what you want to do. It is your responsibility to be the boss *and* the employee. There will be times where you are tested and the question of how much do you want it must be answered. Distractions will present themselves and temptation lurks around the corner. When things get tough – especially when they get tough – giving up, doing something else, not taking action, they all seem so tempting.

Regardless of the situation, never be fooled into thinking that you have no choice. Your ability to choose is one of the few things that is always truly yours. If you believe you no longer have it, then it is because *you* gave it away. If you didn't mean to, then take it back. That's all discipline is; It's holding on to your ability to decide what to do. So no matter what is waiting for you on the path ahead, no matter what happens, always remember you have a choice. You have a choice of what to think, how to feel, what to do, and why you do it.

The 3 Second Rule

Some actions require you to be bold and confident in a single moment. It can be as simple as saying a sentence, but its importance can cause nerves and hesitation. Maybe you want to ask your boss for something, perhaps you want to admit an error to you partner, or maybe you want to tell that beautiful person just how stunning they are and maybe even ask them out. These situations can seem like monumental tasks to some people, but the truth is that we are all capable of doing them. The only thing that can stop you is that little voice in your head.

That little voice has the power to build you up or break you down. If it tends to be the later, then you may notice that its effect builds up over time. You start with a little bit of doubt and the little voice pipes up. "Are you sure? What if it goes wrong? What if they say no, or worse! What if they laugh at you?" Then as time goes on the voice gets louder and the questions become statements. "Don't do it. You will fail. This will not work. You will be humiliated." Before you know it, it isn't even about the action anymore. It is just about you. "You can't do it. You're not good enough. You're a loser. Don't change." What started as a possible action to move forward suddenly becomes a bad idea and then it is used as a weapon to attack your own self-esteem and self-worth.

This mindset can be changed with time. There are coaches who can help train you with this. Self-belief is one of my favourite areas to work in. Empowering people to realise just how much they are capable of. It's amazing to see people breakthrough their own limiting beliefs and become something more.

Another way to get round that little voice is to use 'The 3 Second Rule'. It is a very simple process but it requires you to be bold and trust in yourself. It may not work with the whole action, but it will at least get you to take the first step. Here are the instructions for 'The 3 Second Rule'.

1. Set out a clear instant action you want to take. An action that takes seconds to do.
2. Get yourself in the place or situation to do it.
3. BREATHE. Take some deep breaths.
4. Commit to not breaking The 3 Second Rule. (I like to do a little nod to myself)
5. Count down from 3. 3…2…1…DO IT!

Don't think. Just do it. You already know what you want to do and how to do it, so flick on the autopilot and engage. By using the three second rule, you bypass the little voice by not giving it the time to grow. Counting down and focusing on the numbers with the action helps to drown out anything the little voice does say in the meantime. Give it a try. It is incredible what you can do when you don't talk yourself out of it all the time. Some opportunities don't come around again. Remember this in that moment where you want to do something but hesitate:

**Life isn't made by waiting around
for second chances.
It's made by taking chances in that split second.**

After three seconds, the action is taken and the ball is rolling. After that, it's a lot easier to continue, and if you want to, you can use it again and again until all the actions are complete. Fear and doubt need time to grow and take hold. No time for that, you are too busy making things happen.

Desire vs Mood

Sometimes it is not fear that holds us back from action, but just the lack of drive to do it. We can be motivated to achieve something, yet when it comes to the time of actually doing something about it, we can't really be bothered. It's a conflicting battle between what we want and what we feel. Ideally these two would be the same. However, sometimes they are not. There are times when there is something you plan to do, things that you know you will benefit from, but for some reason you just don't *feel* like doing it. You say things like "I'm not in the mood" or "I can't be bothered". That's ok. These things happen. But before you go off and do something else, take a moment to think about how you are feeling and the result of the action you were planning to take. Ask yourself "Right now, am I operating through desire or mood?"

When we act through desire, we do what it takes to get what we want because we want the outcome of doing it. Even if the thing we have to do isn't fun or exciting, we do it anyway for the result. This is how some people push themselves through the Monday to Friday, nine to five jobs every day. They focus on what having and doing the job brings them rather than the work itself.

When you act through mood, you do what you *feel* like doing in the moment. You feel tired, you rest. You feel hunger, you eat. You have an impulse to go out, you get your shoes and coat, and head out. These are the moments people tend to enjoy most as they are completely present and the action they take feels good because it is what they want right now. Us humans are suckers for instant gratification. When we do what we feel, we get that overall sense of contentment, satisfied with the way the present moment currently is.

As I said, ideally your desire and mood are the same or at least correlate. When they do, you are in the flow and time seems to fly by. However, sometimes there are differences between the two. You may desire an adventurous life of surprises and excitement, but right now you are in a 'stay in' kind of mood. You may desire to finish your project at work, but you feel like going home early and relaxing. You desire to take action but your mood is inaction.

Neither one is right or wrong. I recommend doing a mixture of both from time to time. The important thing is to be aware of the choice and accept what you decide. If you decide not to go out with friends because you feel like staying in, then accept that choice. Don't beat yourself up about it later and make yourself feel bad. You made the choice you wanted in that moment, and if you thought about your desire and mood, then you made that decision consciously.

To operate through desire is to do what you need to do to get what you really want. If you're not sure what that is then ask yourself "If I didn't have to *do* anything, what result would I want?". The answer is what you really want, what you desire. Then the question is 'Do you want to *do* what it takes to get it?'

If you're still not in the mood, the choice of what you do is still up to you. Make a conscious decision and be happy with it. It's what you wanted!

Ecology

The closer you get to the time of taking your action, the more information you will have about what is happening. With this extra information, you are better informed and can make better sense of the situation. Quickly check in with yourself and how you are feeling. Double check the ecology of what you are doing. Be confident that the action you are taking is intended to have the outcome you desire. This is not about doubting yourself or what you are doing. It is about covering your bases in case there is anything you have overlooked. Even if there is and you miss it, it will reveal itself at some point, and when it does you will be ready and you will deal with it.

With every action you take, you are moving closer and closer to creating the outcomes you want in life. Now you are making things happen. What started off as just an idea, just a single thought, is now becoming a reality. You are making life happen the way you want.

Many people think about what it is they want and now you are part of the very small percentage that actually does something about it. Well done for stepping up and doing what it takes.

However, before you start celebrating too much, there is still one more stage before we are done. The final stage to complete the process you have come so far through. Now you have taken action, and maybe even achieved your outcome, we will now revisit where you are so that you can continue your growing success. Due to your action(s), the world and your life are now changing. We must monitor these changes so that you can answer the question "What next?"

Action points:

- Make it easy. Break it down.
- Make a decision and commit.
- Be mindful of your self-talk.
- 'Now' is the only time you can act.
- Know what you want over how you feel.
- Keep it right (ecology).

Eight: Review

"Our past holds many lessons. If learnt and learnt well, we can use them to create a better future."

– Fil Ace Biggs

You have made it to the last stage! Albeit the shortest of all the eight stages, it is no less important. This is where you keep track of your progress, learn from your experiences and maintain momentum. Now that you have done all the preparation and taken action towards your outcome, all that is left to do is to keep going. You may have come to the end of your journey through this book, but for you the story is just beginning. You have merely skimmed the surface of what you are capable of. What you have seen so far is just a little glimpse of what is possible for you.

Reviewing is more than just looking back. There are many benefits to be gained from revisiting aspects of your process in order to get the absolute most for your efforts. We shall go through each one, and in each discover how you can go about getting them. Like an athlete who evaluates their past performance, you are now going to look at what you've done, and with that become a better, more knowledgeable you. Then what you do next can be done even better. Let's go through the benefits of reviewing.

Measuring Progress

We all like to succeed and do well. It can be a drag when we are putting in the hours, the sweat, the grind, but not seeing much result. Sometimes it is because something has to change in the way we do things, sure. However, sometimes it is because the results we are going for come slowly in tiny parts, and this makes them seem invisible. It's like when you see someone you haven't seen for a long time and they have noticeably changed their body size and shape. If you had seen this person every day, then you may not have noticed as much. This is why it is important to have something you can measure in your pursuit to make things happen. That way you can keep track.

Being measurable is something that we covered back in the planning stage. What you measure is up to you. You can measure results, you can measure your efforts, you can measure your effect on the world. Whatever you choose will make an impact on your progress. As Peter Drucker said "What gets measured, gets managed." When you measure progress, you can make it visible. That way it is easy to see how far you have come, and it enforces your momentum to continue.

For example, if you are working on your body, take photos, take tape measurements, keep track somehow. If you are looking at yourself every day, you may not see it. But the measurements will reveal what you cannot see. If you are looking to make money, then measure what you are doing to make your income. Sometimes the measurement you need to see is how much you are putting in, not just how much you are getting out. Or better yet, measure both and find the actions that create the best outcomes. Make your measurements clear and put them somewhere you can see often. A constant reminder of how far you have come and how well you are doing.

Improve

With every action you take, you gain experience and knowledge. This knowledge can only better you if you actually learn it. You can only learn it if you are aware of it. There are potential lessons to be learnt from every experience you have. The successes, the failures (especially the failures), the close-calls, the mishaps, the unexpected results, the changes of plan, the surprising over achievements that turn out a lot better than you expected, they all offer insights that you can learn and grow from.

Every day you move forward, you are no longer the person you used to be. The person you are now is a little bit wiser, a little bit stronger, smarter, confident, motivated, inspired, driven. You are an ever growing sentient being that continues to become more and more with each step you progress forward and upward. Keeping your eyes open to these lightbulbs of wisdom is vital to your own improvement.

Take time to think back on each action you take and how things are going overall. What is going well? What can you improve upon? How can you progress better? What do you know now that will make it easier for you next time? Perhaps you have a lesson for those looking to do something similar. By questioning yourself, you may be surprised to realise just how much you are learning and you may even cause an epiphany of insight that you did not have before. A small piece of extra information that can shift your mind into acting better in the future, from this moment on. Knowledge can be gained from books and teachers, but wisdom is derived from experience. One of my favourite quotes in this matter is from Miles Kington. He said "Knowledge is knowing that a tomato is a fruit. Wisdom is knowing not to put it in a fruit salad."

As you learn from the steps you take on your journey, you are able to offer your teachings to others, and I recommend you do. We all have something special to share and yet sometimes we choose not to. The lessons we learn do us good, but why should we be the only ones who benefit? Both the actions of the most successful *and* the mistakes of the biggest failures have lessons to be learnt. Your successes and mistakes could be someone else's solution. It may even change their lives. Remember, making this happen is about more than just you.

Possibilities

As you change and grow, so does the world around you. Some changes occur as a direct result of actions. When you started this journey, the world was a particular way, and with time new things come into light. With these new things come new possibilities. What was once very unlikely may now be more feasible. The actions you have taken make your final outcome even more likely.

Take a moment to think about the new possibilities for you and your outcome that have arisen as a result of the action(s) you have taken. Your outcome may have been to save £500 to go on holiday, but now that you have taken some action and had some success, you can see how feasible it would be to double that and go to an even better location, or stay in a better hotel, fly business class, do an exciting activity while you're there, or just have more spending money to take. The world changes, your world changes, and so does your attitude. What was once out of sight is now within reach.

This change effects what we can see and what we can envision. Think of it like this. Imagine you are standing in an empty field. You look forward and in the distance you see a city. You look left and see mountains on the horizon. To your right there is the coast and a vast open sea, with a little island placed just within eye sight. From where you stand, you can see all three of these places and so you feel each one is a possible destination for you. Once you take the action to actually go to one of them, your view literally changes. Let's say you go to the city. Now you can see the city in detail and what is in it. The mountains and coast may not be visible anymore but now you have the option of buses and trains that can take you beyond where you can see. You have not changed, just where you are because of the action you took. Now the world around you has changed, and with it, so do the possibilities.

As we grow, so do our minds, and so does our capacity for possibilities. It is no longer about the glass being half full or half empty. Now your glass is growing and you have been constantly filling it. Your potential grows, as does your belief in yourself. Your outlook expands and the world seems as if it is not just changing around you, but it is changing *with* you. Life itself is no longer happening *to* you, it is happening *for* you.

The Danger of Success

Success is great and it is what many of us strive for, but beware of what it brings. Success can be a good thing to go for, but the danger comes once you have it. Happiness and joy come through progression. If you succeed to a certain level and then stop, this will change. It is easy to achieve something and then become complacent with it. Then the effort stops, the progression stops, time keeps going but you do not.

It's like when people go on hardcore diets and workout plans for a few months, then once they get in shape, they go back to their old ways. Or when someone works hard to get out of debt, and then goes back to behaving in the same way that got them into debt in the first place. Results – just like life – requires maintenance. Once you achieve what you set out to do, don't stop. Continue further, higher. Life happens every day. It becomes what you do every day. If you stop progressing, stop appreciating, and stop making things happen, then you stop truly living.

When starting out, we consider ourselves as 'not successful yet'. That is when people put in the work and do great things. The danger of success is that there is no longer that need to put in the work and do great things. So we start putting in little work and achieving average things. If that's what you want, then by all means, go for it. But if right now you're the kind of person who sets out to make things happen then don't let that change. The more you succeed, the more you can succeed. The bigger the things you make happen, the bigger the things you can make happen. Keep growing, keep progressing, and live to the fullest – if you want to.

Desire

This may be one of the most important reviews to do along your path (at least it was for me when I finished university). It is easy to speed forward with blinders on to block out any doubt and distractions, but be aware of moving forward mindlessly. The danger of this is that you are open to being blindsided by the obstacles waiting for you. Some obstacles don't wait for you on the path that you run on. They approach you from the sides and behind so that you don't see them coming. Like Bruce Lee fighting multiple opponents at the same time. Sure you can only attack one (maybe two) at a time, but your awareness is still on where the rest are.

Every so often, be sure to check in with yourself and remind yourself what it is you really want. It has been known for people to pursue big dreams over the length of years, only to achieve what they set out to do and realise it is not what they want anymore. I myself have experienced this. Seven years I walked the path I created to become a secondary school teacher, only to get my degree and realise that it was not what I wanted to do for a living.

If you regularly remind yourself what it is you want and why you are doing this, then you will always be on a path that is good for you because it is the path to what you want. Our desire and intention is what drives our behaviour, and our behaviour is what creates the life we live. Maintaining harmony amongst all parts is a key to creating the life you want. It is imperative to making things happen the way you want them to.

Another danger of being outcome-focused is that you miss out on now. You don't get to fully enjoy the journey you are on. You can't appreciate what you have done or what is happening right now because you never take the time to look back or look around. You may feel like your vision is focused and clear but really you are half blind (maybe more). Like Wild Coyote chasing after Road Runner, you sprint off the edge of a cliff with no idea that you have run out of ground until it is too late. If Wild Coyote had a Coach, he could have been made aware of where the cliff ended, and probably would have made a better way of catching him in the first place.

In a way, this method of looking back is in fact looking forward. Your desire is what you project in front of you. It is what you are moving towards. It can be good to keep your head down and work hard on taking action and achieving goals, but allow yourself some time to glance up every once in a while. That light at the end of the tunnel is the beacon you run for. That paradise in the distance is the final destination of your epic voyage. But what's the point if you're not going enjoy getting there too?

No regrets

When you look back, don't look back with despair or anger, no matter what happens. Once an action is taken, it is done. The past is the past and so looking back on misfortune with regret is a waste of the present. There *will* be times where things do not go to plan. You will make mistakes and wish you had done things differently. Things will go wrong. There are many variables outside of our control.

When these events do occur, it is not time to dwell and point the finger (even at yourself). Know this:

Everything you have done, you did your best with what you had in that moment.

The ability, the knowledge, the attitude, the state you were in, whatever you had at the time, you made decisions and took action with them. When we make mistakes, it is not because we are bad or wrong. It is because we lacked some kind of information, needed more practice, or was not in a state to access our best self. A coach is good for optimising your performance when taking important actions on your journey.

All you do and experience is part of your process. Let go of the way you think things are 'meant' to go, and start acting like you are the one who can *make* things go the way they do. Sure, things may not go quite right, but they are only 'bad' if *you* label them so. In some cases, your growth and development actually require those 'bad' experiences. Regret comes when you assume that an event has now hindered you somehow. It is you who allocates the negative meaning, not the event itself. But what if a so called 'mistake' actually leads to a series of other events that make your life better than ever? What if not being where you planned to be means you end up being somewhere you need to be for something else to happen? Something unexpected but awesome!

Your story is ever being written and you have a say in how it ends. In fact, you're the only one who really has a say. Or at least the final word. The 'Part A' you are going through now may just be the part you need to set up the 'Part B' you want. That's what life is. One big journey made up of many little journeys from A to B. Only time will tell, and with time you can make things happen. The rough seas, the high mountains, the vast desserts, they are all on the way to your final destination. On the way you will learn, you will get stronger, you make a map, and when you arrive you are not just in a different place, you are a different person. Take a look around and take it all in. Breathe in the moment. You've made it happen.

To summarise:

- Measure your progress.
- Make things better.
- Remember what you want (especially if it changes).
- Leave the past and learn from it.
- Keep going!

Epilogue

Congratulations having made it to the end of the process! I hope you have been taking action to make your desired outcome happen. Even if you haven't yet, now you are ready to, and reading this book in itself is an action that has taken you closer, so don't forget that. You have put in the time and effort to make your way through these pages and for that I am very grateful.

Now it is up to you, and to be honest it always was. Don't put this book down somewhere and forget about it. Use it as a manual. Revisit the stages you want whenever you wish, and reveal new insights each time. Or maybe give it to someone else who you feel could benefit from this process to make some things happen in their life.

Let's take a quick look at the stages you have gone through:

- Believe – What you want is possible. You can make it happen.

- Outcome – Know what you want.
- Why – Your reasons are the foundation of making it happen.
- Plan – Bridge the gap between where you are and where you want to be.
- Obstacle – You will have them. Use them.
- Motivation – Get pumped. Get inspired.
- Action – Do it!
- Review – Look back and learn. Improve and move forward.

Now you are 'A Maker'. You are a creator of your life. Your life has been given to you as an opportunity to make it into something you love to live. Everything you want to be, to do, and to have, it's all out there waiting for you. I wish you well on your epic journey and I hope our paths may cross and you can share your own story with me. Maybe I can even help you on your way. Until then, have fun, live consciously, and make the most of life by MAKING IT HAPPEN.

Much love
Fil Biggs

Acknowledgements

Although brief, I believe it is important to give credit where credit is due. First of all, thank you to my mother Ruth for all of your support throughout my life as well as during the writing of this book. You have been a great sound board for ideas and the voice of reason that keeps me focused.

To my friends who have been there throughout the journey, thank you for putting up with me rambling on about the ideas I share in this book and helping me to edit the message being sent so that it is received the way it is intended.

Special mention to Scott Bird (founder of Rising Dragon Martial Arts School). Thank you for providing such a tranquil and serene environment of which most of this book was created. A great place to think and write – as well as train hard. And also for being on the same wavelength when it comes to discussing ideas and possibilities.

A huge thank you to everyone I have worked with in regards to coaching, both professionally and in passing. Every person I speak with presents some kind of insight into how to make things happen. You are my muse. With every problem we solve, our solutions in turn can be used to help others.

Lastly, a huge thank you to everyone who was involved in the publishing process of this book. You have taken my words, my ideas, and helped me to get them into the world by making them into something tangible that can be shared and given.

Thank you all for making it happen.

About the Author

Fil Biggs is a self-improvement life coach known best for his 'to the point' attitude and boundless imagination for possibilities. After qualifying as a secondary school teacher and spending a year training martial arts in China, Fil found his calling when he discovered the area of self-transformation. With the belief that everyone has the potential to do anything, through his own studies he found ways to help people make huge changes in their lives. Since then he has qualified as a Life Coach and Practitioner of Neuro Linguistic Programming.

As well as the hundreds of people Fil has helped already, he continues to spread his message and teachings further and wider, whilst constantly working on his own development to better help more people. His mission is to help over a million people to make positive changes in themselves, in order to create lives they love to live. This book is an example of one of the ways in which he is making that happen.

You can follow Fil on Facebook, Twitter, and Instagram:

- Facebook /TheLifehand
- Twitter @FABiggs
- Instagram @FABiggs

www.lifehand.co.uk